The
Madwoman's
Reason

Nancy J. Holland

The Madwoman's Reason

The Concept of the Appropriate in Ethical Thought

The Pennsylvania State University Press
University Park, Pennsylvania

Library of Congress Cataloging-in-Publication Data

Holland, Nancy J.
  The madwoman's reason : the concept of the appropriate in ethical thought / Nancy J. Holland.
      p.   cm.
  Includes bibliographical references and index.
  ISBN 0-271-01770-8 (hardcover : alk. paper)
  ISBN 0-271-01771-6 (pbk. : alk. paper)
  1. Appropriateness (Ethics)   I. Title.
  BJ1418.5.H65   1998
  170.'42—dc21   97-33170
                                                                CIP

Copyright © 1998 The Pennsylvania State University
All rights reserved
Printed in the United States of America
Published by The Pennsylvania State University Press,
University Park, PA 16802-1003

It is the policy of The Pennsylvania State University Press to use acid-free paper for the first printing of all clothbound books. Publications on uncoated stock satisfy the minimum requirements of American National Standard for Information Sciences—Permanence of Paper for Printed Library Materials, ANSI Z39.48–1992.

To Justis Vincent Koon, a most appropriate child

Contents

Acknowledgments		ix
Preface: The Madwoman's Reason		xi
Introduction: "Once You're Down There, There's No Coming Up": Why Philosophy Must Function Without Foundations		xvii
1	The Concept of the Appropriate	1
2	The Appropriate Past	24
	Interlude: What Is Appropriate Now?	58
3	The Appropriate Present	71
	Conclusion: The Appropriate Future	100
	Bibliography	111
	Index	117

Acknowledgments

The Office of the Dean of the College of Liberal Arts at Hamline University provided substantial support for this project in the form of Hanna Summer Research Grants (1991, 1993, 1994, 1997), course releases supported by faculty development funds (spring 1992, fall 1993), and a sabbatical leave (fall 1995).

As Alison Jaggar has said, "Every book is in some sense a social product."[1] My colleagues in the Department of Philosophy, Duane Cady and Stephen Kellert, provided much needed moral support for this project by reading drafts of chapters and keeping my spirits up during the inevitable dark days. Several colleagues beyond the department, most notably Timothy Polk in religion and Russell Christensen in German, also made important contributions to my thinking. In addition, I would like to thank Sanford Thatcher and the readers for Penn State Press, especially Todd May of Clemson University.

Special gratitude goes to Jeffrey, Gwendolyn, and Justis Koon for their love and patience with a wife and mother whose mind is far too often elsewhere, to the students in my ethics classes over the last fifteen years for their unexpected wisdom, to Brian Mogck for his cheerful commentaries, and to Edythe Alberts for introducing me to the Madwoman.

1. Alison M. Jaggar, *Feminist Politics and Human Nature* (Totowa, N.J.: Rowman & Allanheld, 1983), vii.

Preface:
The Madwoman's Reason

Countess: Heavens! Where do those stairs lead?
Sewer Man: Nowhere.
Countess: They must go somewhere.
Sewer Man: They just go down.
Countess: Let's go see.
Sewer Man: No, Countess . . . once you're down there, there's no coming up.

—Jean Giraudoux, *The Madwoman of Chaillot,* act 2

In Giraudoux's lighthearted diatribe against what some philosophers call "the problem of modernity," Countess Aurelia, the Madwoman of Chaillot, induces the cloned representatives of the modern world—the Presidents, the Prospectors, the Press Agents, and the Ladies—to descend the Sewer Man's staircase to "nowhere," thus ridding the world of the evils they have inflicted upon it.[1] When asked where they

---

1. Jean Giraudoux, *The Madwoman of Chaillot,* adapted by Maurice Valency (New York: Dramatists Play Service, 1947), 40. (Quotations from the play are from this edition, with the page numbers noted in parentheses, unless otherwise indicated.) The original French is somewhat less cryptic that the English (*Giraudoux: La Folle de Chaillot* and *L'Apollon de Bellac* [New York: Dell, 1963], 78):

 La Folle: Où mène cet escalier?
 L'Egoutier: Nulle part. Après soixante marches, on trouve un carrefour en étoile dont chaque chemin aboutit à une impasse.
 La Folle: Je descends voir.
 L'Egoutier: Gardez-vous-en. Les marches sont ainsi faites qu'on les descend facilement, mais qu'on ne peut les remonter.

 —Where does this stairway lead?
 —Nowhere. After sixty steps, there is a star-shaped intersection where every road leads to a dead end.
 —I'll go see.

have gone, she says only that "[t]hey were wicked and wickedness evaporates" (64). Laying aside the strangeness of such a statement in a play that must have been written in occupied Paris,[2] the point remains that the Madwoman made these people "evaporate." Later, she admits her agency in the matter: "Nothing is ever so wrong in this world that a sensible woman can't set it right in the course of an afternoon" (66). At the same time, while the English labels her "the Countess," Giraudoux's text calls Aurelia "la Folle," "the Madwoman," suggesting a more obvious parallel between her "folie" and the madness she has to save us from. The French, in any case, seems to have fewer reservations about the method she uses to save us from it. Where Giraudoux directly points out that the trapped minions of modernity may find rats to eat beneath the streets of Paris but will soon die of thirst, the English is more discreet: "There's only death down there" (40). What, then, is the Madwoman's reason for leading all these "types" to an unpleasant subterranean death? Is it a reason that would be compelling to "any sensible woman"? And what is the relationship between her reason and her madness?

The immediate occasion of the Madwoman's action is an attempt by the President and the Prospector to destroy the city of Paris in order to extract the oil they are convinced can be found underneath it. It is precisely this conviction, in fact, that allows the Madwoman to lure them to their demise. More generally, however, the modern world is described to the Madwoman by the Ragpicker[3] and his "vagabond"

—Don't. The stairs are made so that you can go down easily, but you can't come back up.

(My translation)

I discuss this variation later, but please note in reference to the "original" and the English "adaptation" that Thomas Bishop's introduction to the Dell edition of the French text indicates that several variants existed at the time of Giraudoux's death and that the final French text was established by Giraudoux's producer and collaborator, Louis Jouvet, who also played the Ragpicker in the original Paris production (*Giraudoux: La Folle de Chaillot* and *L'Apollon de Bellac*, 17).

2. The play was the last written before Giraudoux's death in 1944 and was only produced after the Liberation, in December of 1945. It appears, however, to be set in an envisioned postwar world—"the Spring of next year" (5)—rather than in either wartime or prewar Paris.

3. Any resemblance between this Ragpicker and the *Chiffonnier* from chapter 3 of Drucilla Cornell's *The Philosophy of the Limit* (New York: Routledge, 1992) is, of course, not purely coincidental, although the convergence was, in fact, accidental. I came to Cornell's text only recently, several years after I had chosen Giraudoux's

friends, who alert her to the danger, as one in which everything now has a pimp, that is, is brokered through middlemen who take a share of the proceeds without engaging in any productive activity (32). A variant of the same, essentially Marxist analysis is offered by the President, who is upset by the vagabonds' presence in the world: "[T]he only safeguard of order and discipline in the modern world is a standardized worker with interchangeable parts. Here, the manager—And there—one composite drudge grunting and sweating all over the world. Just we two.—Ah, how beautiful! How easy on the eyes! How restful for the conscience!" (18). This last, however, suggests that the problem is as much moral and aesthetic as economic or political. The President goes on to explain why he is so angry at the vagabonds: "My dear sir, wherever the poor are happy, and the servants proud, and the mad are respected, our power is at an end" (18).

It is not so much that the pimps are evil as that they are greedy and therefore stupid (34). They create a world in which there is no longer even the illusion of love between the pimps and what they sell, a world in which "faith [in another man's word] is dead," cut flowers don't last overnight, and pigeons walk because they can't afford to fly. Universal pimping is "the end of free enterprise in this world!" (33). In her efforts to rid us of this evil state of affairs, the Madwoman consults her three friends, the Madwomen of Passy, St. Sulpice, and La Concorde, about the legal and moral niceties of leading those responsible to their doom, which sets the stage for a trial of the miscreants *in absentia*. The "defense" is presented by the Ragpicker, who, told that he is a lawyer and not a witness, swears "to lie, conceal and distort everything, and slander everybody. So help me God" (53). In fact, he takes on the persona of the President to explain how, rather than pursue wealth, he lets wealth come to him. From this flows his power: "Because to have money is to be virtuous, honest, beautiful, and witty. And to be without is to be ugly and boring and stupid and useless." More important, when

---

Madwoman and her accomplices as the touchstone of the present work. Conversely, Cornell makes no reference to Giraudoux, apparently taking the term from Walter Benjamin. Any possible path from Benjamin to Giraudoux would be too convoluted to trace here, but Hannah Arendt did note (in her introduction to the collection of his essays published in *Illuminations*) that Benjamin was very drawn to French intellectual life and in a 1927 letter specifically mentioned Giraudoux, then a novelist, as someone in whose writing "there are certain forces... in which I see at work what occupies me too" (Walter Benjamin, *Illuminations* [New York: Harcourt, Brace & World, 1968], 22).

his proposal to use the oil under Paris to conquer the world leads the Madwoman to call for a guilty verdict, he says, "I am never guilty!" and ultimately, when told to be quiet "in the name of the law," "I *am* the law" (56). Still, the vagabonds find him guilty and authorize the Madwoman to rid the world of the "types" he represents.

The reasons given for her action are thus highly varied: moral ones about the universally corrupting power of money; political ones about the relative power of the nonproductive wealthy and the poor workers (although the vagabonds seem to be more lumpen than proletariat, which I suspect is entirely purposeful on Giraudoux's part); aesthetic ones about the quality of life in the modern world; and romantic ones about the possibility of love. What unites them is an overriding sense that things are wrong and need to be set right. This is not an intuitionistic "sense," however, because much effort is given to showing its intersubjective, if not objective, nature, that is, that it is the result of a consensus among reasonable people (even if some of them are madwomen). Indeed, the audience is invited to become part of this consensus, to applaud and endorse the outcome as they are invited to applaud and endorse Ulysses and Hector's efforts to avert the Trojan War in Giraudoux's more famous play, *La Guerre de Troie n'aura pas lieu (Tiger at the Gates)*. At the same time, however, no effort is made to argue that the morality reflected here is a universal one—the pimps, for instance, would surely disagree. Nor is it a matter of a utilitarian argument overriding a deontological one, since there is no claim that a world cleansed of these "types" will be a happier one in any absolute sense. At the end of the play, there are still pigeons in Paris, but they fly now rather than walk. What, then, is the nature of the Madwoman's reason?

I would like to suggest that the world that the Madwoman and her friends are trying to reestablish is a more appropriate one than the one created by the President and his colleagues. By "more appropriate" I mean here that it comes closer to satisfying an often inarticulate sense of the rightness of things that is shared by a group of people who also share a common culture and many explicit moral values. This culture and these values will underlie the sense of rightness without directly entailing or determining any specific component of it in a way that could be arrived at by logic, unaided by the intuitions developed by membership in that group. Such a group need not have determinate boundaries, and can in some cases be quite large (as large, I would argue, as European Christianity or the common law tradition) or quite small (as small as the student body at a liberal arts college), but the values of larger groups will generally place certain limitations on what can count as appropriate for smaller groups within them. (Traditionally, for instance, the United States has tolerated a variety of religious practices without endorsing those that deny such toleration to other religions.) This concept of appropriate behavior within specific contexts is also intended to serve as a critical tool that could be used to evaluate the concrete practices of a given tradition, without accepting the validity of all such practices based simply on their current, noncritical relationship to that tradition, but also without importing any external standards of moral evaluation. Such critical thought, however, can emerge only from within the tradition itself.

Thus, I would argue, Giraudoux can appeal to the shared values of an educated, tolerant public tired of war for support of the judgments of appropriateness made by the Madwoman and her friends even in the absence of an argument based on explicit moral principles. Indeed, he hints, any such argument could favor the other side—"I am the law," says the Ragpicker/President. Please note, however, that this appeal to the appropriate is not an appeal to feminine "care" in lieu of masculine law or "justice" (although I argue later that the account of the appropriate here is inherently feminist). Indeed, the Madwoman's claim is that she is acting on behalf of "justice," and her actions are far from caring ones. My argument follows, rather, in an often "masculinist" tradition that runs through Marx and Nietzsche to Foucault and beyond, a tradition well known to Giraudoux. This tradition suggests that rationalization is often (always?) in the service of those in power. As I argue elsewhere, the insistence on systematic reason over what seems appropriate and on rules over emotion may be, historically and geographically, very specific to high Western European culture.[4] Thus my claim is broader than the context of gender differences in Eurocentric societies, and instead suggests ways in which we might understand and respect cultural differences regarding what is morally appropriate without falling into a relativism that would render us unable to critically evaluate the specific judgments made by other cultural groups, or relying on a universalism that would deny them their own historical specificity.

Perhaps the Madwoman was wrong to do what she did. The relative

---

4. See my "Opinions of Men and Women: Toward a Different Configuration of Moral Voices," *Journal of Social Philosophy* 24, no. 1 (1993): 65–80.

coyness of the English version of the text suggests a certain discomfort with it, at least. The French relies more on an aesthetic sense of rightness than on a moral one, and American audiences are famously reluctant to replace moral judgments with aesthetic ones.[5] On the other hand, in the 1960s milieu in which I first encountered the Madwoman (as the Flower Girl in a high school production), we tended to see the aesthetic case being made as a logical one: reason generated the madness of (the possibility of nuclear) war; therefore what madwomen and "street people" endorsed must be good. I think now, however, that Giraudoux was more subtle than that. Reason could not prevail against Nazism, against modernity in its ultimate form, but there was something very wrong with that modernity, something deeply inappropriate about the world it created for itself and its opponents. *The Madwoman of Chaillot* is a call to see something other than the modern world, not something older or more pure, but something more appropriate, which is to say, finally, something more beautiful, more comfortable, and more human.

---

5. This may explain why Jean Renoir's luscious film of this play—starring Katherine Hepburn as the Madwoman and Danny Kaye as the Ragpicker—fell without a ripple into the pool of American cinema. Perhaps if the film had been as exciting as, say, *Pulp Fiction,* instead of merely technically perfect, its moral ambiguity would have been less of a problem for audiences.

Introduction

"Once You're Down There, There's No Coming Up":
Why Philosophy Must Function Without Foundations

The scene in which the Madwoman of Chaillot lures the "types" of the modern world to their doom in the labyrinthine sewers of Paris is literally a scene *mise en abîme*. Their subterranean demise, properly offstage, cannot be securely grounded in any Kantian Universal or utilitarian benefit, in any Platonic Goodness or Aristotelian virtue. It is merely an appropriate response to the degraded modernity they have created. Or so it seems to a group of madwomen and vagabonds. But what ground or reason is there to speak of this destructive act as an ethical obligation, or even to speak of reason here at all? Reason, like the law, seems geared to produce a result that favors the "types." As Jean-François Lyotard says of moral and legal obligation alike: "The obligated one is caught in a dilemma: either he or she names the addresser of the law and exposes the authority and sense of the law, and then he or she ceases to be obligated solely by the mere fact that the law, thus rendered intelligible to cognition, becomes an object of discussion and loses its obligatory value. Or else, he or she recognizes that this value cannot be exposited, that he or she cannot phrase in the place of the law, and then this tribunal cannot admit that the law obligated him or her since the law is without reason and is therefore arbitrary."[1] What intelligible discourse could provide the law for the obligation under which the Madwoman acts?

Better, perhaps, to ask what discourse could provide the law or the obligation for any act that would call itself ethical. The history of modern philosophy is the history of the end of history, the end of the so-called metanarrative(s) that tell us what history means, what our lives mean, what our actions mean.[2] Since at least the sixteenth century (some would say since Scotus and Ockham in the thirteenth and fourteenth centuries),[3] the history of philosophy has been the slow deconstruction of the foundations of ethical justification, both metaphysical foundations and those that would offer themselves as nonmetaphysical, whether naturalistic or logical.[4] And although, since at least the thirteenth century, the history of this deconstruction has tended to divide itself along the English Channel, geography has not proved to be ultimately decisive on this point. Anglo-American philosophy might have reached is (anti)apotheosis a bit more quickly than its Continental counterpart(s), but it might also have taken longer after the fact to recognize the situation for what it was.

What it was, of course, is "the end of metaphysics." The fact that the recognition of the impossibility of irrefutable "first principles" is of so little interest to almost everyone in itself seems to validate the claim that metaphysics is at an end: we no longer even notice its absence.

---

1. Jean-François Lyotard, *The Differend: Phrases in Dispute,* trans. Georges Van Den Abbeele (Minneapolis: University of Minnesota Press, 1988), 117.

2. Of course, what I am about to construct is also a "metanarrative" of a sort, as is much of Martin Heidegger's work in the history of philosophy. The difference in these two cases, or in Heidegger's at least, is the absence of meaning-giving, or rather the giving of the absence of meaning, or perhaps the giving of the meaning of absence: "The history of being is the '*Geschick*' of being that proffers itself to us in withdrawing its essence" (Martin Heidegger, *The Principle of Reason,* trans. Reginald Lilly [Bloomington: Indiana University Press, 1991], 61).

3. I would not have trusted my own sense that these two names are relevant here, if not for the similar sentiments alluded to in John Caputo's *Against Ethics* (Bloomington: Indiana University Press, 1993).

4. As is often the case in both Continental and ordinary language philosophy, I have been trained to regard any foundational claims as *prima facie* metaphysical, so I will not address the possibility of a nonmetaphysical foundationalism, although an implicit criticism of such approaches may emerge in what follows.

What causes more people to take notice is its necessary consequence: "the end of ethics." Traditionally, ethics, or *phronesis* (practical wisdom), has been understood to rely on higher-order principles about the goals of human life, which were themselves based on the claims about the nature of reality and reason that constituted metaphysics (or more recently on claims about the natural world or the limits of practical reason). While I argue in Chapter 2 that this historical metanarrative itself is not entirely true, it is still the case that, in the Christian era at least, how one was supposed to act was highly dependent on what one understood God to be, that is, on one's basic metaphysical commitments. As God becomes more distant and more abstract in the history of Western philosophy during the modern period, this traditional basis for ethical judgment, the metanarrative that justified moral rules in terms of duty and salvation, also slowly recedes.

The "godless" (post)modern world, this world after the "end" of metaphysics, is the world in which the Madwoman of Chaillot must find the means to save the way of life that she and her friends consider worth living. The lack of any foundation, metaphysical or otherwise, on the basis of which she might justify her actions, any "reason" for her actions in the traditional sense, leaves her with no choice but to save her world through an *abıme ex machina*. Here I will try very briefly, very roughly, to sketch the history of that abyss, on both sides, in order to clarify the problem to which this work is intended to provide a possible solution.

From Slim to None: Nonfoundationalism in Anglo-American Philosophy

John Locke stands at the center of "modern" Anglo-American metaphysics as he does at the center of modern Anglo-American political thought. Although he was an empiricist, in the British tradition, Locke's metaphysical dualism was in many ways similar to Rene Descartes's.[5] Whereas Descartes relied on our "innate" ideas of Self, substance, and causality to provide the basis for his proof of God's

---

5. John Locke, *An Essay Concerning Human Understanding*, ed. John W. Yolton (New York: Dutton, 1961), 2:221.

existence, Locke first refutes any claims to innateness, then uses their shared dualism itself as the basis for his own proof. Locke begins, as does Descartes, with our own (material) existence and uses a first-cause argument to move from there to a most powerful eternal being. He then adds the fact of our perception and knowledge (i.e., mind) to generate the attribute of "most knowing" for this eternal being, and goes on to say of it that "whether anyone will please to call [it] *God,* it matters not."[6] While such a conception of God is very compatible with the deism of Locke's political heirs in the North American colonies, it is notably unhelpful in the making, or grounding, of ethical judgments in the absence of a religious doctrine that might give this abstract God the necessary moral qualities. This is one reason Anglo-American political liberalism has come to entail, if not deism, at least neutrality among concrete religious and moral beliefs.[7]

At least partly in reaction to such political, religious, and moral "freethinking," George Berkeley sets about proving the existence of a far more concrete, biblical deity,[8] but at considerable cost. As an empiricist, Berkeley is unable to draw upon Descartes's doctrine of innate ideas to flesh out his conception of God, and does so instead by denying what seems most metaphysically self-evident: the existence of the body half of Locke's mind/body dualism. By denying the existence of matter, Berkeley is able to reduce us to limited minds under the guidance of an infinite mind (i.e., God) whose qualities are sufficiently like our own to justify our reliance on what we learn of Him through the Bible. Thus a grounding for ethical judgment in God is achieved by eliminating material substance, one of the traditional components of the metaphysical grounds for believing in God. Note that there is also a diminution of the claim to universal reason as a ground here. Whereas reason, and hence a "deistic" ethics, is understood by Locke and his colonial followers to be an attribute of men qua men (*sic*), acceptance of the Bible as the ground for our ethical understanding of God would, in this period, exclude from the moral realm not only nonbiblical religions but also

---

6. Locke, *An Essay Concerning Human Understanding,* 2:219, emphasis in the original.

7. On this point, see, for instance, Charles Taylor, *The Ethics of Authenticity* (Cambridge, Mass.: Harvard University Press, 1991), and Alison M. Jaggar, *Feminist Politics and Human Nature* (Totowa, N.J.: Rowman & Allanheld, 1983).

8. George Berkeley, *Three Dialogues Between Hylas and Philonous,* ed. Robert Merrihew Adams (Indianapolis: Hackett, 1979), 5.

Catholicism, to the extent that authority and reason remained paramount over revelation.

David Hume took a long slide down the slippery slope that Berkeley had thus introduced into the grounds of Locke's system. The antiskeptical skepticism Berkeley uses to eliminate material substance Hume turns against a range of other "metaphysical" entities, most famously causal necessity, free will, and, almost parenthetically, mental substance, or the Self.[9] Religion is here moved completely out of the sphere of reason and into the realm of "miracles."[10] Ethics, on the other hand, is moved into the empirical realm; that is, it is transformed into a sort of descriptive utilitarianism explained in terms of what is *"useful, or agreeable* to a man *himself,* or to *others."*[11] Hume's ethics fails to be fully utilitarian for the same reason that it is "merely" descriptive— because it is lacks any clear claim to a universal, rational basis. Instead, each nationality seems to be free not only to judge how the useful or the agreeable is to be achieved, but also to judge, to a certain extent, what will count *as* useful or agreeable.[12] God and universal ethical foundations always disappear hand in hand.

What allowed British philosophy to pass another century without full recognition of the ethical abyss opened up by Hume's "mitigated" skepticism was a detour that later came to be called "the naturalistic fallacy," that is, normative utilitarianism. The basic attempt of this position, which is discussed more fully in Chapter 2, was to ground moral judgment in empirical (social) science. With a renewed, if no better grounded, faith in causal explanation, the scientism of the classical utilitarians allowed them to argue from the fact that people did desire pleasure to the conclusion that pleasure was desirable. Even while admitting that this argument is really no argument at all,[13] John Stuart Mill and others use the production of pleasure and the reduction of pain as the grounds for moral, and political, judgment. That the

---

9. See the appendix to David Hume, *A Treatise of Human Nature,* ed. L. A. Selby-Bigge (Oxford: Oxford University Press, 1975), 633–36.

10. Hume, *A Treatise of Human Nature,* 474. Compare Hume's *Enquiry Concerning Human Understanding,* ed. Eric Steinberg (Indianapolis: Hackett, 1977), 90.

11. David Hume, *Hume's Enquiries,* ed. L. A. Selby-Bigge (Oxford: Oxford University Press, 1975), 336, emphasis in original.

12. On this, see both the "Dialogue" in *Hume's Enquiries,* 324–43, and Hume, *A Treatise of Human Nature,* 614–21.

13. John Stuart Mill, *Utilitarianism,* ed. George Sher (Indianapolis: Hackett, 1979), 34.

measures and meaning of pleasure and pain could be culturally variable was something to which they paid some attention, only if often to argue it away. Whether one might be systematically (self-)deceived about what caused pleasure or pain, on the other hand, is not a question they seriously consider. What, then, are we to make of Giraudoux's "types," who prefer oil wells in their backyards to almond trees? Marxism would probably have an explanation for the inappropriateness of their desires, but classical utilitarianism, it seems, might not—unless it could count them as "perverts," along with the inhabitants of the infamous, if mythical, "society of sadists."

While retaining its nineteenth-century scientism, Anglo-American philosophy in the early twentieth century seems to return to a more Humean position with regard to metaphysical and ethical thought. For logical positivism, neither metaphysics nor ethics, much less God, belong to the philosophical realm any more at all. Language about all three is shunted aside as "merely" emotive, without referent and hence also without meaning.[14] All variants of this emotivism in the analytic literature (intuitionism, prescriptivism, etc.) have two major implications. The first, and the more interesting to the analytic philosophers themselves, is that emotive moral judgments are not subject to evaluative argumentation. That is, one might argue with someone about whether an action such as ethnic cleansing was correctly described as one of "murdering the innocent," but since moral judgment is a matter of emotion, one could not rationally argue that murdering the innocent is wrong with someone strongly inclined to believe that it is not. The second major implication, which is more relevant here, is an obvious cultural relativism. Different cultures, traditions, and life experiences will generate different emotions, intuitions, and prescriptions for correct action. The Humean ethical abyss between and within cultures has reopened beneath our feet, leaving (social) science as the only arbitrator of moral and political choice.

Even the residual metaphysics inherent in the scientism of logical positivism, however, is undermined by the more radical linguistic philosophies of J. L. Austin and Ludwig Wittgenstein. Austin points out that the positivists' claim to eschew metaphysics and to replace it with a language of "sense-data" only masks a deep commitment to

14. For one classical statement of these claims, see A. J. Ayer, *Language, Truth, and Logic* (New York: Dover, 1952), especially chaps. 1 and 6.

traditional metaphysical materialism.¹⁵ He also joins Wittgenstein in questioning the possibility of a "pure," context-free language of sense-data that could serve as the foundation for science, or presumably for any "scientific," that is, naturalistic or logical, system of ethics.¹⁶ Rather than "language" or "logic," Wittgenstein speaks of "language games" and emphasizes their failure to provide a basis for absolute claims. "You must bear in mind that the language-game is so to say something unpredictable. I mean: it is not based on grounds. It is not reasonable (or unreasonable). It is there—like life."¹⁷ For Wittgenstein, the moral consequences of this groundlessness can seem to echo positivistic emotivism—"At the end of reasons comes *persuasion*" —with more unfortunate echoes to follow—"(Think what happens when missionaries convert natives)."¹⁸ Thus, in the end, the effort to replace God and ethics with language and science as the foundation for judgment, as possibly envisioned by Hume and carried out by the logical positivists, fails. Only the abysmal play of language games remains to justify the Madwoman's act.

Which Side Are You On? Nonfoundationalism in Continental Philosophy

Since a large part of Chapter 2 is devoted to Immanuel Kant's attempt to reinstate the possibility of morality in the face of Hume's abyss, I will take the liberty of omitting the first two hundreds years or so of modern philosophical thought in the rationalist tradition and start instead with a quick preview of Kant's (temporary) synthesis of Anglo-American and Continental philosophy. The greatness of that synthesis consists in redefining the mind/body split in terms of an interaction between the external world and human faculties that gives us knowledge of the experienced world, or phenomenal realm, without allowing us full access to the noumenal realm of intelligible being. At the same

---

15. J. L. Austin, *Sense and Sensibilia*, ed. G. J. Warnock (Oxford: Oxford University Press, 1979), 106–7.
16. See, for instance, Austin, *Sense and Sensibilia*, 76.
17. Ludwig Wittgenstein, *On Certainty*, ed. G.E.M. Anscombe and G. H. von Wright, trans. Denis Paul and G.E.M. Anscombe (New York: Harper, 1972), 73e.
18. Wittgenstein, *On Certainty*, 81e.

time, Kant dissolves the empiricism/rationalism split by introducing the possibility of a priori synthetic judgment, which recaptures the content of Descartes's innate ideas in a way that can be seen to evade Locke's counterarguments. What this is intended to generate is an epistemology and a "grounding for the metaphysics of morals" that will ultimately return God to the realm of rational discourse, at least at its margins in the noumenal. This position shares with classical Anglo-American liberalism one feature that proves decisive in the history of colonialism in the nineteenth century: universal reason is central to the possibility of ethics, whether it is Kantian "practical" reason or the instrumental reason of utilitarianism. Knowing in advance, from reason alone, what others truly want, or what our duties toward them are, makes it far easier to ignore the concrete demands they may make of us.

It is not surprising, therefore, that European liberalism traces its roots back to Kant via the work of G.W.F. Hegel, who, like Locke, did philosophy with one eye on the political crises of his time. Metaphysically, Hegel goes Kant one better by having a positive, if not strictly theistic, concept of God. His idea of God is one that had lain hidden in the philosophical shadows since the work of Locke's rationalist contemporary, Baruch Spinoza. On this view, "[w]hat is rational, is actual, / and what is actual is rational,"[19] where the rationality in question is, ultimately, the mind of God. While metaphysically quite complex, this identification of God with the real has at least one interesting moral consequence. In Hegel's metanarrative, as reality evolves according to this inherent rationality, morality and the legal demands of the liberal political state come to coincide with each other and with the will of God, thus allowing us to justify the state because it promotes a universal morality (much like Kant's), while at the same time allowing us to ground that morality in the laws of the (liberal, democratic) political state.[20] As in the transition from Locke to Berkeley, the role of God has become much greater, as has the specificity of belief required (here Lutheran, there Anglican), while the connection to our experienced reality, which makes Locke's and Kant's positions so compelling, is to

---

19. G.W.F. Hegel, *The Encyclopaedia Logic*, trans. T. F. Geraets, W. A. Suchting, and H. S. Harris (Indianapolis: Hackett, 1991), 29.

20. On this point, see chap. 4 of Drucilla Cornell's *Philosophy of the Limit* (New York: Routledge, 1992).

a large extent lost. Such a rationalized system may be more optimistic and satisfying than deistic abstractions, but can also be correspondingly less persuasive in the face of the crises of actual human life.

Karl Marx, on the other hand, champions human life over Hegelian, or capitalist, rationalizations. At the same time, he also rejects liberalism's other nineteenth-century face, utilitarianism, as both insufficiently deep in its analyses of economic phenomena and insufficiently compassionate in the face of the evils of capitalism. While economically and politically worlds apart, Marx and Hume share two attributes that are central to the present discussion. First, in the wake of a predecessor intent on minimizing, if not denying, the reality of the material world, Hume and Marx both work, each in his own way, to reassert the importance of matter, and of a certain kind of science, in any reasonable account of human experience, even to the extent of questioning the role of consciousness, or an abstract Self. Second, in the wake of powerful theistic claims, they go beyond the deism that lies behind them to entertain, in Hume's case, or assert, in Marx's, full atheism. Moreover, they are both willing to accept the inevitable ethical implications of their religious suspicions. The good is redefined in each case in ways that are relativistic, independent of any universal reason, and even potentially nihilistic.[21] They flirt with Fyodor Dostoyevsky's nightmare of modernity from *The Brothers Karamazov*, the fear that, in the absence of God, "everything is permitted." The fate of Soviet "Marxism" in the twentieth century perhaps only proves the dangers of such flirtation.

Whereas the abyss Hume opened with his skepticism is bridged over to a large extent by the utilitarians, the Marxist abyss is only deepened by the even more powerful suspicion of Friedrich Nietzsche. Nietzsche is the perfect anti-utilitarian, seeming to be the champion of elitism, aristocracy, and needless pain, the enemy of the masses, comfort, and moral values—but, of course, only "seeming to be." Nietzsche deepens the chasm that runs along the English Channel by becoming the stylistic nemesis of generations of Anglo-American professors and editors who search endlessly through papers by artistic students and articles by Continental philosophers, wanting to know "where's the argument?"

---

21. For one statement of the relationship between Marx's materialism and his ethical relativism, see Karl Marx, *Selected Writings*, ed. David McLellan (Oxford: Oxford University Press, 1977), 172.

The substitution of style for a rationality that has been perverted into instrumentality enacts the very lack of grounds for justification for which Nietzsche is "arguing." As in logical positivism, moral choice is a matter of taste, of emotion, and God is long since dead. Nietzsche lacks the positivists' commitment to science as a replacement for God; he is clearly discontent with the world the way it is, clearly another critic of modernity. He would probably agree with the Madwoman about almond trees and oil wells, but he would surely reject putting her action to a vote—the Sewer Man and the Ragpicker would offend his famous sense of smell.[22] The Madwoman's argument, moreover, is no more simply an appeal to style than it is an appeal to "higher men," and Nietzsche's nihilism, while compatible with the destructiveness of her act, would give her no basis for preferring pigeons that fly to ones that walk.

Continental philosophy does, however, make one small detour in its march to the metaphysical/ethical abyss. The "linguistic turn" in twentieth-century Anglo-American philosophy has a rough analogue in the brief, but highly influential, history of structuralism in Continental thought. Elaborating on their empirical data, the structuralists sought to replace the decayed foundations of metaphysics with a network of meanings that, while groundless piece by piece, could generate a structure strong enough to provide some (quasi-)scientific basis for moral and political choice. Thus, Jean Piaget wanted his structural theory of child development to be the impetus for educational reform, and Claude Levi-Strauss uses his understanding of the structure of myths as the basis for his diatribe against Jean-Paul Sartre's Hegelian/Marxist idea of "peoples without history."[23] As in utilitarianism, the social sciences were to be used to rationalize the process of ethical and social decision making, while, as in logical positivism, the data to be used were primarily linguistic, or quasi-linguistic, rather than material in nature. The consequences of structuralism are likewise mixed: morality is present, but as a sidelight on the scientific advances to be gained from this new methodology.

The history of structuralism is short because the center could not

---

22. See, for instance, Friedrich Nietzsche, *The Portable Nietzsche*, trans. and ed. Walter Kaufmann (New York: Viking, 1968), 408.

23. See chap. 9 of Claude Levi-Strauss, *The Savage Mind* (Chicago: University of Chicago Press, 1966).

hold. That is, for structuralism to provide a ground for choice, even a suspended one, it required some necessary connection between the structures it created and the material world in which choices are acted out. While never denying that such connections existed, poststructuralist thought quickly pointed out that there was no necessity to those connections, and so no grounding for the grounds that structuralism might provide: "Rather, it is a question of determining the possibility of *meaning* on the basis of a 'formal' organization which in itself has no meaning."[24] Like the "pure" language of sense-data that was the Holy Grail of logical positivism, a structure in which any sign always represented any one other sign or any one external reality would always be undermined by the effects of context and of the language games themselves.[25] Drawing on resources that range from Marx to Austin, poststructuralist thinkers celebrate as play the very groundlessness that many would see as a problem. While aware of the dangers of "the end of ethics," they seem to see no alternative to its relativism and nihilism, except perhaps in small, local actions based on deep respect for context and the demands of the Other. What follows is the working out of one dimension of exactly this aporia of postmodern ethics.

"Where Do We Go From Here?"

Thus, whether the Madwoman stays within the confines of the Continental tradition that she, and Giraudoux, inherited from Kant and Hegel, or seeks answers from the Anglo-American tradition that seems to provide at least some of the mottoes of the "types" to whom she is opposed, the great mainstream Western philosophical traditions cannot provide any solid grounding for the reasons she needs to save her world from the ravages of modernity. As Jacques Derrida points out, the Transcendental Ideas of Pure Reason central to the great Kantian synthesis have each fallen prey to the intellectual revolutions of the

---

24. Jacques Derrida, *Margins of Philosophy,* trans. Alan Bass (Chicago: University of Chicago Press, 1982), 134.
25. See the classic argument of Jacques Derrida's "Structure, Sign, and Play in the Discourse of the Human Sciences," in his *Writing and Difference,* trans. Alan Bass (Chicago: University of Chicago Press, 1978).

last century: the Psychological Idea to Freud, the Cosmological Idea to Einstein, and the Theological Idea to Darwin.[26] The Madwoman seems to be reduced to presenting a pastiche of justifications for her condemnation of those she would destroy, and to rely on a vote of vagabonds and madwomen finally to determine their fate. The first question to be addressed in what follows is whether this irrationalism is irreducible. Despite the lack of metaphysical foundations for her argument, can the Countess still have reasons for what she does, good reasons, reasons that count?

What I hope to have shown in the preceding overview of certain structural similarities in the two main traditions of modern Western philosophy is that the question of grounds and reason is invariably tied up with the question of relativism. In these traditions, universal moral grounds based on universal human reason generate universal values, which in the absence of such universals can be seen as sentimental illusions, at best, or imperialistic rationalizations, or worse.[27] At the same time, as the recent romanticism about traditional cultures recedes, certain practices in these cultures come to the fore that could almost make us wish for the days when there were good reasons for asserting Western values in the non-Western world. Primary among these is the practice of clitoridectomy and genital mutilation used in certain traditions as a way to guarantee chastity in women. For me, this is the ultimate test case of any ethical system, relativism explicitly included. Of course, there is no strictly logical reason for giving this particular human evil primacy—surely many things are more painful, more destructive, less respectful of human life or human rationality. Still, there are reasons that can tell us how deeply inappropriate it is permanently to deprive a human being of sexual pleasure, to cause a woman untold amounts of unnecessary pain simply in order to control her sexuality more effectively.[28] While I talk of the Madwoman here,

---

26. Jacques Derrida, *Specters of Marx*, trans. Peggy Kamuf (New York: Routledge, 1994), 97.

27. In the second category, see, for instance, Mill's limitations on liberty for colonized peoples (*On Liberty*, ed. Elizabeth Rapaport [Indianapolis: Hackett, 1978], 10) and Hegel's argument against the participation of Asian philosophies in "world history" and hence in the liberal moral consensus (see chap. 4 of *Introduction to the Philosophy of History*, trans. Leo Rauch [Indianapolis: Hackett, 1988]).

28. My colleague Duane Cady has pointed out to me how inadequate the word "inappropriate" seems in this particular context. I retain it for two interrelated reasons. First, the present discussion is intended to function at the level of the

this more agonizing case is always in the shadows, the case of sane women deprived of the joy of their own bodies for perfectly "good" reasons.[29]

The argument in favor of the concept of appropriate action as a cross-cultural criterion for moral choice implicitly demands that it exclude ritual clitoridectomy as an acceptable practice, but the details of that exclusion must be left to those with a far deeper understanding of the traditions in which it is practiced. What I can offer here is only the general, formal argument for a critical use of the concept of what is appropriate, based on the deepest sources of any given tradition, and hope that my faith that the more specific case can be made on this basis is justified. This is what Heidegger believes to be the very nature of the philosophical enterprise: "Philosophy can and must define what in general constitutes the structure of a world-view. But it can never develop and posit some specific world-view qua just this or that particular one."[30] At the same time, the objection has been raised that my faith in the ultimate formal similarity and "fairness" of all cultural systems is only a postmodern version of the old imperialistic faith in a universal human reason.[31] If so, if even the deepest understanding of

---

kind of "ethical theory" I hope to justify in the Conclusion, rather than at the level of moral judgment, so that a vocabulary of inappropriateness is more strictly correct than one that would express more accurately my moral outrage. Second, in discussing the customs of other cultures, judgments couched in terms such as "inappropriate" might serve precisely to keep moral outrage from interfering with the real-world possibility of making preliminary steps toward the cultural reinterpretation that would be necessary actually to eliminate such moral horrors.

29. Some have accused American feminists who refer to the practice of clitoridectomy of sensationalizing this tragic problem, but I believe that Gayatri Spivak is closer to correct when she says that an "at least symbolic clitoridectomy has always been the 'normal' accession to womanhood" (Gayatri Chakravorty Spivak, "Displacement and the Discourse of Woman," in *Feminist Interpretations of Derrida*, ed. Nancy J. Holland [University Park: Pennsylvania State University Press, 1997], 67). This can be seen in far less extreme form in the European tradition: for example, in the Freudian claim that "mature" female sexual pleasure was centered on the vagina rather than the clitoris. In any case, while this example serves as one extreme of the argument, I will refer to it only rarely, in order to avoid seeming to exploit the human pain it represents.

30. Martin Heidegger, *The Basic Problems of Phenomenology*, trans. Albert Hofstadter (Bloomington: Indiana University Press, 1982), 10.

31. This point was first made in conversation by Lucius Outlaw, but Lyotard also refers to it when he says that in finding that traditional narratives, and cultures, "'already' have a cosmopolitan 'import,'" one is engaging in a genre of discourse that "'already' has universal human history as its referent." He notes

the traditions in which it is practiced fully justifies the sexual mutilation of little girls, I will be proved wrong about the concept of the appropriate. Nothing could ever convince me that I am wrong about the evil of the practice itself.

The argument proceeds in three stages. The first begins with a full development of the concept of the appropriate, based primarily on the work of Martin Heidegger. Respectful of Jacques Derrida's critique of Heidegger's use of the concepts of the appropriate and appropriation, however, I recast the concept of appropriate action in a way intended to evade at least some of Derrida's criticisms. To make my case crosscultural as well requires an attempt to uproot the concept of the appropriate from the Greco-German soil where Heidegger lodges it. In order to achieve both these ends, the argument returns to premodern thought, so the second stage is a step backward to look more closely at how ethics is tied, or not tied, to metaphysics in the work of Aristotle and Kant. If, as I hope to show, these classical ethical systems in fact rely more on a sense of the appropriate than on any more solid metaphysical foundation, it would seem that the approach described here may also provide a viable basis for ethical judgment.

There follows an interlude in which I seek to apply the concept of the appropriate, so defined and delimited, to the question of the ordination of women in the Roman Catholic Church, as a sort of privileged example. The third stage of the argument is a comparison of the view developed here with three major areas of contemporary nonfoundational ethical thought: virtue theory, postmodernism, and feminist ethics. The claim is that a critical use of the concept of the appropriate provides better reasons for the kind of the moral decision that the Madwoman is forced to make than any of these alternatives. Indeed, that may be the only kind of argument we can have: "Our discussion will be adequate if it has as much clearness as the subject-matter admits of, for precision is not to be sought for alike in all discussions."[32]

What will all this prove? Three things. First, that in making moral

---

that this can be called "projection," but says that he "would prefer to call it a begging of the question" (Lyotard, *The Differend*, 156).

32. Aristotle, *Nicomachean Ethics*, trans. David Ross (New York: Oxford University Press, 1980), 2–3.

decisions that go beyond the usual bounds of ethical thought, the best criterion for judgment would be a sense of what would be the appropriate choice to make under the circumstances, based on the deepest possible understanding of the tradition to which one belongs and in which one lives. This seems to be what the Madwoman does when she consults the other madwomen in deciding what to do about the representatives of evil in the modern world. Second, that this is all that the great systems of ethics have ever told us and is in fact what makes the systems of Aristotle and Kant arguably more significant contributions than the more consistent moral teachings of their contemporaries, because it allows their ethical beliefs to be translated into different metaphysical and cultural contexts. Finally, that this is also how we should judge the ethical choices and cultural practices of those whose traditions are not the same as ours—that is, that we should hesitate to judge them at all without as deep an understanding of the appropriateness of those choices and practices as thoughtful participants have available to them. The advantage of such a quasi-formal approach to ethical theory would lie in its ability to acknowledge contextual variation across cultures while holding the ideal of appropriate behavior constant. No Absolute Law based on God and Universal Reason here, no nihilistic relativism, but rather a hope for more appropriate actions based on a deeper understanding of human existence in particular historical and social contexts. Nothing more, and nothing less.

1
The Concept of the Appropriate

> Going where it is possible to go would not be a displacement or a decision, it would be the irresponsible unfolding of a program. The sole decision possible passes through the madness of the undecidable and the impossible: to go where ... it is impossible to go.
> —Jacques Derrida, *On the Name*

While my argument in this book is largely based on the work of Martin Heidegger, in ways that should become clear in this chapter, the idea of using the concept of appropriate action as a form of moral evaluation did not have its origin in Heidegger or even, strictly speaking, in philosophy at all. Rather it grew out of a life experience in which the moral and the aesthetic often seemed to merge in a way that led me to reconfigure aspects of both in terms of the appropriate. This can be traced back to sources such as popular culture over the last thirty years—"God don't like ugly"; "The local team won, but it wasn't pretty"—and the sayings current in my social circle over roughly the same period of time—"If you weren't beautiful, then you would have to be good"; "Not appropriate, Holland" (as a general expression of disapproval). This reconfiguration began to become a philosophical issue when I learned in an interdisciplinary faculty seminar that the biblical concept of "righteousness" was a relational one, that is, that it had to do with what was appropriate to a specific relationship.[1] It is in this sense that Rebecca was the appropriate, or righteous, wife for Isaac, as well as beautiful (to him) for that reason. Later I read a colleague's book on rhetoric in which he argues that irony can only be understood on the basis of some previous sense of what is appropriate.[2] Well schooled in the moral uses of irony in both Socrates and Søren Kierkegaard, I began to see that something important might be hidden in what had so far been only a personal choice to reformulate certain moral decisions into quasi-aesthetic judgments of appropriate action.

Many years of studying the work of Jacques Derrida, however, led me at once to the relationship between the appropriate and what is or can be appropriated. This unfortunate connection, which is even more unfortunately derived from a shared etymology, underscores further links between the appropriate and property, and between all of these concepts and the French *propre* (what is proper, in the sense of morally or socially acceptable, but also what is one's own). When I began to look at Heidegger for some more philosophical understanding of the concept of the appropriate, I found that these same resonances existed in German between *eigenst* (ownmost) and *Eigentlichkeit* (authenticity) in *Being and Time,* and *Ereignis* (event) and *geeignet* (appropriate) in his later work, so he offered no easy solution to the problem that deconstruction posed for me. At the same time as it exposed this problem in my thinking, however, Derrida's work suggested the path to its solution. Perhaps it would be possible to re(con)figure the difference between what we appropriate and what is appropriate as a sort of diffe*ra*nce, an invisible difference similar to the silent "a" of differance.[3] What I hope to establish in this chapter is, in Derrida's terms, that the invisible diffe*ra*nce between the appropriate and what we appropriate is a telling diffe*ra*nce, one that ultimately might tell, unexpectedly, in Heidegger's favor rather than Derrida's.[4]

---

1. See Timothy Polk's "In the Image: Aesthetics and Ethics Through the Glass of Scripture," *Horizons in Biblical Theology* 8 (1986): 27–59.

2. See Donald Rice and Peter Schofer, *Rhetorical Poetics* (Madison: University of Wisconsin Press, 1983), 30–33.

3. In fact, Derrida himself suggests such a maneuver with regard to the French word *plus,* which can mean either "more" or "no more," depending on whether the final *s* is pronounced or not. See his *Gift of Death,* trans. David Wills (Chicago: University of Chicago Press, 1995), 100.

4. Charles E. Scott, *The Question of Ethics* (Bloomington: Indiana University Press, 1990), covers, under the heading "Dasein's most proper being," much of

The Event of Appropriation

If coming down on the side of Heidegger in this exposition is unexpected, perhaps his mere presence here is even more so. Still, the links that tie the family of words that includes such important concepts as *eigenst* (ownmost) and *Ereignis* (literally, "event," but a very complex concept in the later Heidegger) to very basic quasi-ethical concepts such as *Eigentlichkeit* (authenticity) can be traced throughout his work.[5] And the links between that Germanic chain and its Latin counterpart in what is both appropriate and proper are clear. What follows is, therefore, an exploration of the configuration of concepts in Heidegger's work that leads from the appropriate through appropriation and authenticity to Albert Hofstadter's translation of *Ereignis* as the "disclosure of appropriation" and finally to Heidegger's concept of the appropriate as a gathering together of human existence.

1

It might be best to begin in the middle, with a brief summary of Hofstadter's linguistic point about the links from *eigenst* to *Ereignis*. He argues in the introduction to *Poetry, Language, Thought* that the use of *Ereignis* in "The Thing" plays on its etymological relationship to *eigen* to shift its meaning from "event" to "appropriation, making one's own," and specifically to the mutual appropriation of the fourfold of earth, sky, mortals, and divinities.[6] Thus, in a schema closely related

---

the same territory that I do here, but he does not engage in any extended consideration of either a deconstructive or a feminist critique of the Heideggerian text.

5. In "The Letter on Humanism" Heidegger denies any moral relevance to the concept of authenticity, but he does not recommend inauthenticity, even if he may regard it as inevitable, so I will take authenticity to be a quasi-moral concept (Martin Heidegger, *Basic Writings*, trans. David Farrell Krell [New York: Harper, 1993], 236). (In a footnote to this paragraph, Krell retranslates *Uneigentlichkeit* [inauthenticity] as "inappropriateness.") Robert Bernasconi also argues for the quasi-moral status of authenticity, based on Heidegger's lectures on the Aristotle in *Plato's "Sophist"*: "In spite of everything Heidegger will later say in *Being and Time* to take the discussion of authenticity and inauthenticity out of the sphere of the ethical, these passages give further reason for doubting if this is possible, at least in respect of ethics in the Greek sense" (Robert Bernasconi, "Heidegger's Destruction of Phronesis," *Southern Journal of Philosophy* 28, supplement [Spindel Conference, 1989]: 134).

6. Martin Heidegger, *Poetry, Language, Thought*, trans. Albert Hofstadter (New York: Harper, 1975), xix.

to the four causes in Aristotle, the jug that Heidegger describes in "The Thing" is composed of clay (earth) formed by human (mortal) hands, according to the idea of what a jug should be (sky), into a vessel that can be used for libation (to the divinities). What brings this fourfold together is that each is destined for the others, becomes most what it is in serving, or being appropriated to serve, the needs of the others. What is proper to the existence of the fourfold is their mutual appropriation, and from this process arise both things and events in the usual sense. Thus, appropriation, the mutual making one's own of the fourfold, is central to understanding the later Heidegger's concept of Being itself.

Hofstadter also notes, however, an intermediary stage in this evolution from *eigen* to *Ereignis:* the verb *eraugnen* (to place before the eye), which he relates in turn to Heidegger's concept of the "lighting" or the "clearing" (*die Lichtung*).[7] The "clearing" is the space in which human existence appropriates (or is "sent" or "given") specific things, events, and truths as objects of explicit awareness, against a background of unthematized consciousness, as the eye might see objects in a clearing in the forest against an undifferentiated background of trees, a background that also defines (or "gives") the clearing itself. It is in this "clearing" that things can become what they are, through the "gathering-appropriating staying of the fourfold."[8] The 1956 addendum to "The Origin of the Work of Art" also ties the "clearing," or the Open, retroactively to *Ereignis*, conceiving of art as "disclosive appropriation."[9] Similarly, in his translation of "The Turning," William Lovitt cites the sentence *"Ereignis ist eignende Eraugnis"* and translates it as "Disclosing coming-to-pass is bringing-to-sight that brings into its own,"[10] or, roughly, "The event of appropriation is a bringing into view that thereby brings into its own."

What might justify the attempt to link this chain of concepts from

---

7. Heidegger, *Poetry, Language, Thought,* xx-xxii. My colleague Russell Christensen reports that the Grimm brothers insist that *ereignen* shows a corruption of the diphthong *au* or *eu* to *ei* and so is unrelated to *eigen*. This would support Hofstadter's link between *Ereignis* and *eraugen,* but only by denying the more important point about the relationship to *eigenst.* Hofstadter, however, notes that Heidegger approved his translation of *Ereignis* (xxi), so the Grimms are apparently not the final authority.

8. Heidegger, *Poetry, Language, Thought,* 174.

9. Heidegger, *Poetry, Language, Thought,* 86.

10. Martin Heidegger, *The Question Concerning Technology,* trans. William Lovitt (New York: Harper, 1977), 38.

the "later" Heidegger to an early work such as *Being and Time,* beyond the superficial etymological connections with *Eigentlichkeit?* At the very least, *Being and Time* seems to use the puns provided by this linguistic family to tie together quite fundamental concepts. To cite just one such chain, the category of the appropriate appears central to an understanding of the "authenticity" of the ready-to-hand, that is, the equipment and other objects around us, which are generally invisible to us in their everyday use. As such, these objects cannot be completely unready-to-hand, or unavailable for use, but only, "at worst, appropriate for some purposes and inappropriate for others."[11] Heidegger's logical chain here first links the ready-to-hand to what is appropriated (*zugeeignet*), then points out that the ready-to-hand has the peculiarity (*Eigentumliche*) that it can be authentically (*eigentlich*) ready-to-hand only when it withdraws from thematic consciousness, that is, only when it is invisible because used in the appropriate way.[12] Thus, the key to understanding the category of the ready-to-hand lies in its relationship to a sense of the appropriate object or action that is very similar to the latent awareness of what is appropriate in language that licenses the moral possibility of irony. Both of these references to what is appropriate, in turn, show it as functioning in much the same way as the background, or Open, of "The Origin of the Work of Art"— all based on a linguistic chain that corresponds to the links between authenticity and the appropriate in English.

To take another case, the section on truth in *Being and Time* calls for Dasein to "explicitly appropriate what has already been uncovered, defend it *against* semblance and disguise, and assure itself of its uncoveredness again and again."[13] For Heidegger, truth as *aletheia* is not a present-at-hand objective reality or correct representation that could simply be opposed to something false, but is always a disclosure against a constant background of what is hidden. Truth is discovered within the always partial "clearing" of human existence. So, "Dasein is equiprimordially both in the truth and untruth,"[14] and the appropria-

11. Martin Heidegger, *Being and Time,* trans. John Macquarrie and Edward Robinson (New York: Harper, 1962), 115.
12. Heidegger, *Being and Time,* 98–99.
13. Heidegger, *Being and Time,* 265, emphasis in the original.
14. Heidegger, *Being and Time,* 265. Compare the claim in *Plato's "Sophist,"* which was written about the same time, that for Aristotle "speech (*logos*), in its very sense, is at first neither true nor false" (Martin Heidegger, *Plato's "Sophist,"* trans. Richard Rojcewicz and Andre Schuwer [Bloomington: Indiana University Press, 1997], 124).

tion of what is disclosed in this sense is the way in which Dasein makes truth its own. In Division Two of *Being and Time,* as well as in "The Origin of the Work of Art," this means that "[r]esoluteness appropriates untruth authentically."[15] Again, Heidegger seems to exploit the links between the authentic, the appropriate, what is appropriated, and what is one's ownmost, *propre.*

2

At the other end of this linguistic chain, *Ereignis* seems not to be used with its usual meaning in *Being and Time,* as Hofstadter suggests it is, but rather is used specifically in a negative sense, as a "mere" event, most often something that happens as part of the "historical," in the usual (or Hegelian) sense of the term.[16] Conversely, the argument is made several times that death is *not* such an event. In "Time and Being," at the other end of Heidegger's career, the meaning of this term has been completely and explicitly reversed—and tied once more to the appropriate and its cognates: "*Ereignis* will be translated as Appropriation or event of Appropriation. One should bear in mind, however, that 'event' is not simply an occurrence, but that which makes any occurrence possible."[17] Here *Ereignis* is related to Being itself, as the process by which both things and events in the usual sense come into the "clearing" of human existence. Moreover, the title of this piece, as well as its references to specific passages from *Being and Time,* strongly suggest that the transformation of this concept in the development of Heidegger's thought is due to a purposeful major rethinking of its possibilities and resonances, rather than merely a specialization of its use.

It is in "The Turning," however, that two small clues appear that suggest that the change in Heidegger's understanding of the appropriate and the appropriated is less complete and more subtle than it

15. Heidegger, *Being and Time,* 345. For "The Origin of the Work of Art," cf. *Poetry, Language, Thought,* 67.
16. Thanks are due here to the translators of *Being and Time,* John Macquarrie and Edward Robinson, for apparently knowing people might be interested in Heidegger's early use of the word *Ereignis* and indexing it for us, although it bears no special weight in the text they were translating.
17. Martin Heidegger, *On Time and Being,* trans. Joan Stambaugh (New York: Harper, 1972), 19.

may at first appear. There, Being is described as "that which genuinely [*eigentlich*] is."[18] Lovitt presumably translates this in a way that masks its relationship to authenticity in *Being and Time,* because the Being referred to here is very different from the being of Dasein (although the German sentence is given in a footnote). In the later Heidegger the focus has shifted precisely from Dasein, human existence, to Being itself, so the appearance here of a term so central to the hermeneutics of Dasein in *Being and Time* may be meant to underscore the difference between the two uses of the word, and hence the two texts in which they appear, rather than be an invitation to confuse them.[19] The *eigenst* that is at issue in this text is no longer the ownmost of Dasein, but rather the mutual appropriation of the fourfold. *Ereignis* is that event of appropriation, and so it is Being itself that is *eigentlich* ("authentic").

The role of mortals, that is, Dasein, in this authenticity is, moreover, the result of a denial of human agency, the result of our appropriate appropriation by the fourfold: "Only when man, in the disclosing coming-to-pass (*Ereignis*) of the insight by which he himself is beheld, renounces human self-will and projects himself toward that insight, away from himself, does he correspond in his essence to the claim of that insight. In thus corresponding man is gathered into his own (*ge-eignet*) that he, within the safeguarded element of the world, may, as the mortal, look out toward the divine."[20] When we are gathered into what is our ownmost, that is, appropriate (*geeignet*), we become part of the mutual appropriation of the fourfold, part of that which authentically is, and hence become again ourselves authentic. As this circle of concepts closes, the distance from *Being and Time* to "Time and Being" begins to seem very small indeed. Perhaps that is part of the point. This configuration suggests that authenticity, the ownmost (*eigenst*) possibility of Dasein, the truth disclosed in the clearing of Being, and the *Ereignis* of the fourfold as mutual appropriation can

---

18. Heidegger, *The Question Concerning Technology,* 44.
19. In "The Thing," moreover, death plays a role in the definition of mortals very similar to the one it plays in the definition of Dasein in *Being and Time* (Heidegger, *The Question Concerning Technology,* 178–79).
20. Heidegger, *The Question Concerning Technology,* 47. Please note that English transforms a neuter noun here into a masculine concept and so turns us all into men, and it is also the translator, not Heidegger, who makes the explicit move from what is appropriate (*ge-eignet*) to what is one's own.

function as quasi-moral concepts, or at least as recommended ways of being, closely related to a concept of appropriate action.

What this means in relation to the ethical use of the concept of the appropriate is that just as our unthematized understanding of how the hammer works is invisible in our ready-to-hand use of it, and just as the truth that underlies our understanding of Being becomes invisible, is hidden as *aletheia,* so our normal sense of appropriate action is invisible in our everyday acts of moral judgment. On this account, our sense of what is appropriate would become visible or explicit only when our ready-to-hand use of it, its hiddenness, is blocked in some way that makes morality "unready-to-hand," or problematic. If traditional approaches to unblocking the process fail, the underlying "rule" of appropriate action may become "present-to-hand" as an object of thematic consciousness that we can choose to accept or to reevaluate, but in full knowledge that there can be no grounding for such reevaluation is any transcendental, "objective" reality. We become "authentic" for Heidegger in our choice of action under this condition of indeterminacy, in our conscious appropriation (or rejection) of what we previously accepted uncritically in our immersion in the everyday. On this view, one of the "objects" given shape and meaning in the Open created by the Greek temple, along with "trees and grass, eagle and bull, snake and cricket,"[21] would be the moral structure of the world the temple created, a moral structure we can see being made explicit, and evolving, in the work of the classic Greek tragedians.

This last result is similar to the transformation of ready-to-hand tools such as the lever and the inclined plane into unready-to-hand objects of large-scale engineering problems eventually resolved into present-to-hand formal mathematical and physical principles. In the same way, the explicit thematization of traditional moral values when unusual problems arise places them in relationship to each other and thus always potentially makes obvious the inconsistencies, the contradictions, among them. This critical function is central to my use of the concept of the appropriate. The lesson in *The Madwoman of Chaillot,* however—and Heidegger's lesson in his work on technology—is that these two critical processes are similar, but not identical. The thoughtful, reflective comparison of the values implicit in our sense of the appropriate, like the thoughtful, reflective understanding of literature

---

21. Heidegger, *Poetry, Language, Thought,* 42.

or the thoughtful, reflective understanding of the meaning of Being, is an art, not a science. Instrumental rationality has its (cultural, historical) limits, the limits of the law personified by the Ragpicker/President. Just as Heidegger's recasting of metaphysics reveals the limits of science and any epistemology of the "merely" present-to-hand on which it may be based, so calling on the concept of the appropriate reveals analogous limits in the moral realm and brings forward the need for authenticity, the need to supplement the law with a deeper sense of human value.

Deconstructing the Foundation

Of course, finding the Heideggerian roots of the concept of the appropriate does not necessarily argue in its favor. Any feminist discourse that takes as its privileged example a play written in occupied Paris must find a National Socialist, no matter how reformed and rehabilitated, a very strange bedfellow indeed. Nor is the incongruity entirely adventitious. When one harkens back to the history of Western philosophy, as Heidegger often does, one also harkens back to a time when women, and other Others, were more oppressed in more ways in more places than they are today. It is the *self-critical* use of tradition, the appeal to a perhaps deeper sense of what is appropriate conduct toward the Other/others, that I want to invoke here. As Heidegger says, with perhaps more self-confidence than is entirely appropriate, "We not only wish to but must understand the Greeks better than they understood themselves. Only thus shall we actually be in possession of our heritage."[22] Such a hermeneutic appeal to the deepest sources of a tradition may be the basis, at least in part, for whatever makes so obvious the bad faith of those who use a more superficial, or a more contaminated, reading of ancient texts to justify oppression as part of their ethnic and religious heritage, whether that heritage comes from the furthest periphery of the modern world or the supposedly core "family" values of Western European Christianity.

The self-deconstruction of even the most banal of such arguments

---

22. Martin Heidegger, *The Basic Problems of Phenomenology*, trans. Albert Hofstadter (Bloomington: Indiana University Press, 1982), 111.

follows in structure the far more sophisticated critical readings of Heidegger found in Derrida's work. And much of his criticism of Heidegger, and other authors, centers precisely on the chain that links the appropriate to the appropriated and the *propre*. In *Specters of Marx*, Derrida says of Marx's "Eighteenth Brumaire of Louis Bonaparte" that the "whole anachronistic dislocation plays in the inadequation between the phrase and the content—the *proper* content, the appropriate content. Marx believes in it."[23] Marx believes in an "appropriate content," uses it as the basis of his heavy-handed irony, in the way described above. Derrida implies, on the other hand, that he does not believe in it, although surely he believes in, and subscribes to, the irony. Why he does not believe in an "appropriate content" can be traced back to his very early work on Heidegger and the links he draws there between authenticity and the *propre*, based on the relationship between *Eigentlichkeit* and *eigenst* in *Being and Time*.

1

At least one manifestation of this argument, in "*Ousia* and *Gramme*," is part of an attempt to show a continuity of thought between Aristotle, Kant, and Heidegger that, while quite different from the one that will be traced here, might suggest at least a formal similarity between Derrida's thinking and my own. The different valuation we might each put on any underlying continuity between the three philosophers is tied to one of Derrida's main contentions in this paper—that the link between authenticity and the *propre* created by moving from German to French shows a tie between the authentic in Heidegger and what is "near" (the Latin *proprius*). This chain of concepts then moves to what is present and, according to Derrida, ties both Aristotle and Heidegger (and Kant as one intermediary between the two) to the metaphysics of presence. The appropriate would also fall under this censure because Derrida's critique "can propagate its movement to include all the concepts implying the value of the 'proper.'"[24] What is proper to us or most our own, what we appropriate, is what is near to us, and so to

---

23. Jacques Derrida, *Specters of Marx*, trans. Peggy Kamuf (New York: Routledge, 1994), 115, emphasis in the original.
24. Jacques Derrida, *Margins of Philosophy*, trans. Alan Bass (Chicago: University of Chicago Press, 1982), 64.

value *it* is always also to value presence as both the present moment and what is present to us, the present-to-hand, as the primary, yet privative, mode of the modern understanding of Being. Since both Heidegger and I would reject the link between what is appropriate or authentic and the value of the present-to-hand, Derrida requires a reinterpretation of the first part of this formulation that would eliminate, or weaken, the link between them.

In another of his relatively early readings of Heidegger, "The Ends of Man," Derrida also links the "proper of man" and presence in order to suggest a residual, if quite complex, humanism in Heidegger's work. Moreover, this version of the argument is closely linked to my own concerns here because it is framed by Derrida in reference to "the violent relationship of the whole of the West to its other, whether a 'linguistic' relationship ... , or ethnological, economic, political, military relationships, etc."[25] The project is again both to underscore and to question the continuity between Heidegger's thought and the traditional metaphysics from which he seeks to distance himself (in this case, Hegel and Husserl). Thus Derrida says that "in the *Letter on Humanism* and beyond, the attraction of the 'proper of man' will not cease to direct all the itineraries of thought.... It is in the play of a certain proximity, proximity to oneself and proximity to Being, that we will see constituted, against metaphysical humanism and anthropologism, another insistence of man, one which relays, relieves, supplements that which it destroys, along pathways on which we are, from which we have hardly emerged—perhaps—and which remain to be examined."[26] For Derrida, any appeal to what is appropriate to "man" seems much the same as an appeal to the metaphysics of presence and the definition of the human that it traditionally entails.

A footnote later in "The Ends of Man" follows the same etymological chain I have been tracing in support of Derrida's argument for a continuity of Heidegger's thought in this area: "The motif of the *proper* (*eigen, eigentlich*) and the several modes of *to propriate* (particularly *Ereignen* and *Ereignis*), both of which thematically dominate the question of the truth of being in *Zeit und Sein*, has long been at work in Heidegger's thought."[27] Through its links to proximity, he then follows

25. Derrida, *Margins of Philosophy,* 135. (This text carries the not inconsequential date of May 1968.)
26. Derrida, *Margins of Philosophy,* 124.
27. Derrida, *Margins of Philosophy,* 129n (italics as in the original).

this chain back to the fourfold, and to the immediate neighborhood of the appropriate—"Now this presence of the fourfold, in turn, is thought, in *On Time and Being* notably, according to the opening of propriation as the nearness of the near, proximation, approximation" —and finally to Being itself—"Propriety, the co-propriety of Being and man, is proximity as inseparability.... The proper of man, his *Eigenheit*, his 'authenticity', is to be related to the meaning of Being."[28] Thus Derrida notes much the same continuities in Heidegger's work that I have outlined, and draws rather similar conclusions about their relationship to a quasi-ethical understanding there. By linking them to the problem of foundations and the metaphysics of presence, however, through the chain that moves from the proper to proximity, he sees this continuity in terms of a limitation on Heidegger's thought, rather that in terms of its potential to open that thought to a rethinking of nonfoundational ethics.

2

In *Specters of Marx*, roughly twenty years later, the focus of Derrida's work has shifted somewhat from a concern with the metaphysics of presence to a more explicit concern with the links tying authenticity and the proper to appropriation, in the literal sense, and to property. Another change over the same period of time has been some lessening of Derrida's tendency to equate ethics more or less immediately with what he earlier called the "ethicotheological"[29] and an increasing awareness of the need to keep open the possibility of moral judgment despite the impossibility of providing a transcendental foundation for it. The question he poses for himself in *Specters* is that of learning to live, which he terms "ethics itself," but an ethics linked to the political and a future, rather than a present, time.[30] On this basis, however, he continues to consider as on the other side of whatever new reality he envisions that aspect of Heidegger's work that I have adapted for my own use.

The old argument reappears fairly early in *Specters*, beginning with a critical reading of the event (*Ereignis*) in Heidegger and elsewhere

---

28. Derrida, *Margins of Philosophy*, 133.
29. See, for example, Derrida, *Margins of Philosophy*, 45.
30. Derrida, *Specters of Marx*, xviii-xix.

but then moving to justice and Heidegger's reading of the Greek *dikē* as a justice beyond the law, not, perhaps, unlike the one invoked by the Madwoman herself. Such justice, however, would be a gift, Derrida notes, a present, an exchange item, something that was once the property of the giver but now becomes the *propre* of the recipient. Justice so conceived—and Derrida strongly suggests that Heidegger so conceives it—would then fall back within the metaphysics of presence (or of presents, as it were), whereas *dikē* would seem to be precisely that which is outside of such a system of exchange. "Otherwise justice risks being reduced once again to juridical-moral rules, norms, or representations, within an inevitable totalizing horizon (movement of adequate restitution, expiation, or reappropriation).... To be 'out of joint,' whether it be present Being or present time, can do harm and do evil, it is no doubt the very possibility of evil. But without the opening of this possibility, there remains, perhaps, beyond good and evil, only the necessity of the worst."[31] This is, of course, precisely the dilemma posed by the Madwoman, but it is less clear that the move, or evasion, that Derrida attributes to Heidegger's attempt to avoid this dilemma is itself entailed by the values, the sense of the appropriate, that Heidegger and the Madwoman (and perhaps Derrida) seem to share.

Toward the end of this text, the same chain of concepts is invoked against Marx in what I would consider one of Derrida's less persuasive arguments, and perhaps tellingly so. In a characteristic attempt to undo dualism, Derrida is concerned to question the distinction in Marx between the use-value and the exchange value of objects. He does so, however, by linking Marx's argument to a humanism both he and Heidegger would have transcended, and thus to the property, the properties (*Eigenschaften*), and the *propre* of man.[32] He then ascribes Marx's belief in "pure" use-value to yet another nostalgic search for a time before culture, before the corruption of exchange and commodification: "Just as there is no pure use, there is no *use-value* which the possibility of exchange and commerce ... has not in advance inscribed in an *out-of-use*—an excessive signification that cannot be reduced to uselessness."[33] At the same, Derrida is quick to note that there is no "pure" exchange value either, that he is not suggesting or promoting

---

31. Derrida, *Specters of Marx*, 28–29.
32. Derrida, *Specters of Marx*, 150.
33. Derrida, *Specters of Marx*, 160, emphasis in the original.

the commodification of everything, because, reciprocally, use-value also always already contaminates the capitalist system of exchange. "If capitalization has no rigorous limit, it is also because it comes itself to be exceeded."[34] He then returns to his original concern with the event, in this case the "apparition" of exchange value.

In these pages, Woman makes her own apparition on the scene. One of the first lessons of (post)structuralism was the necessity of the commodification of women, our exchange value in the binding together of society.[35] This proves, on the one hand, that what would seem to be most outside the system of exchange—the most intimate relationships of individuals—is, in fact, the very condition of its possibility. If women (but is it a question here of women or of Woman?) have no "pure" use-value, then what indeed could? On the other hand, since the "impure" use-values represented by women/Woman continue to exist as such even under the highest forms of capitalism, then this spooky apparition of the primordial/Woman has not been totally exorcised from the modern world, which is also part of Derrida's point.

My point, as one such ghostly remnant, is that the system of exchange has never captured, can never capture, the full use-value of interpersonal relationships or the new lives they can produce. These might well represent, instead, exactly the "pure" use-value Derrida would deny—a use-value perhaps less pure or primordial than irreducible. My own body has use-value for me; however, it might be perverted into an exchange value or a commodity as well, either for myself or others. Perhaps the extent of that perversion is part of the deep evil we sense in slavery, prostitution, or the genital mutilation of girls—the transformation of a "pure" use-value into an exchange value that not only erupts into our experience of that use-value from an all but absolute exterior, but also inevitably destroys it in the process. Human bodies and their sexuality can be, often are, bought and sold, but that only proves that even at the extremes use-values can become exchange

---

34. Derrida, *Specters of Marx,* 163.
35. Claude Levi-Strauss, *The Elementary Structures of Kinship,* trans. James Harle Bell, John Richard von Sturmer, and Rodney Needham (Boston: Beacon Press, 1969). See also the important feminist commentaries by Gayle Rubin ("The Traffic in Women," in *Toward an Anthropology of Women,* ed. Rayna R. Reiter [New York: Monthly Review Press, 1975]) and Luce Irigaray (*This Sex Which Is Not One,* trans. Catherine Porter [Ithaca, N.Y.: Cornell University Press, 1985]) with special emphasis on the relationship between Marx and Levi-Strauss on this issue.

values or commodities, not that they were never anything else.³⁶ My daily family life shows me that they *are* something else. The same is probably true for Derrida. The question is what philosophical weight to give the phenomenology of the "everyday" that is so significant as a starting point for the early Heidegger and of such value to the Madwoman and her friends.³⁷

But the "everyday" in Heidegger—Derrida would be, indeed was, among the first to point out—is not my "everyday" of family life. This would just be another example of the phenomenon he cites in *Given Time,* which dates from the decade between *Margins* and *Specters:* "[N]ote that we say between men, apparently *between men,* both in the sense of humanity and of masculinity, and of a humanity better represented, as always in this examplarist logic, by the example of men than by that of women."³⁸ Derrida, in contrast to Heidegger, offers himself here as the friend of Woman, or perhaps of women. Many contemporary feminists, however, are wary of this gift of friendship. A large part of their reluctance lies in the perception that postmodern thought in general, and Derrida's work in particular, by denying them access to the intellectual legacy of the Enlightenment, also denies them the tools they need to enact an emancipatory feminist intellectual and political project.³⁹ Of course, few of these feminists would consider Heidegger's work any more suitable for this project than Derrida's. But if the move to nonfoundationalism outlined in the Introduction is to carry any weight, such a response to the arguments here would seem to offer feminism the same choice offered us by Hume, that between "a false belief and none at all."⁴⁰ We cannot go back, not

---

36. On this issue in *Specters of Marx,* see also Gayatri Chakravorty Spivak, "Ghostwriting," *diacritics* 25 (summer 1995): 66–68.

37. For a more general discussion of the devaluation of the use-values produced by women in Marxist thought, see Nancy C. M. Hartsock's classic article, "The Feminist Standpoint: Developing the Ground for a Specifically Feminist Historical Materialism," in *Discovering Reality,* ed. Sandra Harding and Merrill B. Hintikka (Dordrecht: D. Reidel, 1983).

38. Jacques Derrida, *Given Time: I, Counterfeit Money,* trans. Peggy Kamuf (Chicago: University of Chicago Press, 1992), 115, emphasis in the original.

39. For more on this topic, see *Feminist Contentions: A Philosophical Exchange* (New York: Routledge, 1995), with papers by Seyla Benhabib, Judith Butler, Drucilla Cornell, and Nancy Fraser, and an introduction by Linda Nicholson, and *Feminist Interpretations of Derrida,* ed. Nancy J. Holland (University Park: Pennsylvania State University Press, 1997).

40. David Hume, *A Treatise of Human Nature,* ed. L. A. Selby-Bigge (New York: Oxford University Press, 1975), 268.

back to the Enlightenment and not (despite what I have to say on the subject below and in the next chapter) back to the Greeks. The future is inevitable, and the path seems to me to lead, for the moment at least, through, rather than around, both Heidegger and Derrida.

Reappropriating the Appropriate

If women, or Woman, is the locus of the irrational in modernity and in Western culture as a whole, as well as in Giraudoux's plays, then my archeology, retrieval, or reevaluation of what appears to be irrational in the moral use of the concept of the appropriate may well be inherently feminist, as well as feminist in its aim.[41] In this sense, madwoman would be a redundancy. And for the same reasons, Heidegger's archeology, retrieval, reevaluation, and retranslation of ancient Greek philosophical texts is of significance here less because they are Greek than because they are ancient. The persistence of these texts into the modern age, unmediated by any continuous religious tradition to serve as a bridge between their world and ours, provides perhaps our only access to what is Western and yet not modern. Not that we can ever retrieve these texts in their wholeness, or even approach it, but they can suggest to us, as they do to Heidegger, what is hidden in our own history in a way that can illuminate the limits of the modern. Unlike Heidegger, I would put no value on the Greek as Greek, much less as proto-German, but I do value what we can learn from the Greeks about alternative ways of living within the Open that they have given us.[42] The full exposition of what I think can be learned from Aristotle about the appropriate will be developed in the next chapter, but for now I would like to follow the slender trail of only one word in the Aristotelian text, not surprisingly one that I believe can be retranslated in terms of appropriate action.

41. On this, see Sara Ahmed's "Beyond Humanism and Postmodernism: Theorizing a Feminist Practice," *Hypatia* 11, no. 2 (1996): 71–93.
42. For a similar use of ancient Greek texts, though one based on an entirely different philosophical enterprise, see Bernard Williams's *Shame and Necessity* (Berkeley and Los Angeles: University of California Press, 1993), 3 and throughout. (Note that Williams rejects Gary Brown's translation of Nietzsche's *unzeitgemass* as "unmodern" in favor of the traditional "untimely"—even though "unmodern"

The perhaps more surprising transition from Derrida to Aristotle is authorized, as it were, by Derrida himself, twice and seemingly in two directions. *Given Time* notes that five different Greek nouns can be translated as "gift," and that "Aristotle speaks of . . . a gift that, for once, would not require restitution. The importance of this allusive citation is in truth beyond measure. It announces the link between the economy of the proper, appropriation, expropriation, exappropriation, and the coming or the coming-back of the event as restitution or beyond restitution, in the *Ereignis* or in the *Enteignis*."⁴³ While Derrida clearly wants to enclose Aristotle—and Heidegger—within the circle of the proper and the economy of its variations by noting that only one kind of gift escapes this circle, he must do so precisely by telling us that Aristotle can *still* speak of a gift beyond the economy of the restitution of the proper. Perhaps this importance "in truth *beyond* measure" would trace a line between a feminist ethics of appropriate action that would exceed the demands of justice as the law of the economy named here by Aristotle and an other economy that may well have appropriated his proper name only much later and further West, in the name of the Law. A law of reason, a justice that would always exclude the Madwoman's reasons, would expropriate all that Woman/women represent in the world opened up by that law.⁴⁴

1

What would be appropriate for Aristotle? In the *Nicomachean Ethics*, moral excellence, like *aretē* in any *technē*, is governed by a law of proportionality: "The master of any art avoids excess and defect, but seeks the intermediate and chooses this."⁴⁵ What provides this proportion for practical wisdom (*phronēsis*) is *sōphrosunē*, a link that Aristotle justifies, in good Heideggerian fashion, with a questionable

---

suits his own purposes better—because he fears the contamination of the term "unmodern" by the "fashionable" term "postmodern" [170 n. 6].)

43. Derrida, *Given Time*, 81.

44. This is not to suggest, of course, that Aristotle or the ancient Greeks in general had better things to say about women, merely, perhaps, that they had very different things to say. For a fuller explanation of the cultural/historical claim alluded to here, see my "Opinions of Men and Women: Toward a Different Configuration of Moral Voices," *Journal of Social Philosophy* 24, no. 1 (1993): 65–80.

45. Aristotle, *Nicomachean Ethics*, trans. David Ross (New York: Oxford University Press, 1980), 37.

etymology roughly equivalent to a move directly from the appropriate to proportionality in English.[46] While *sōphrosunē* is often translated as "temperance," it functions in Aristotle more as a standard of proportional, that is, appropriate, behavior. For instance, Alcibiades praises Socrates as a *sōphron* in the *Symposium,* where their drunkenness makes "temperance" an unlikely translation.[47] On this view, moral virtue would be a matter of acting appropriately in various situations, or the ability to enact excellence in different contexts, and *sōphrosunē* in this sense would bear roughly the same relationship to the specific virtue of temperance that justice as "complete virtue" does to justice in the narrow sense.[48] Such a distance between *sōphrosunē* and temperance is also suggested by Terence Irwin in the notes to his translation of the *Ethics,*[49] and by Gilbert Murray, who translates the word as "temperance, gentleness, the spirit that in any trouble thinks and is patient, that saves and not destroys."[50] For Murray, proportional or appropriate behavior, the excellence of *sōphrosunē,* was a central value for the Greeks in general, as well as a major virtue for Aristotle in particular.

Why does the name of Aristotle enter into this achronology, and especially enter on the side of Heidegger?[51] Much earlier, in *Writing*

---

46. Aristotle, *Nicomachean Ethics,* trans. Ross, 143. Among others, Heidegger, in his discussion of the *Ethics* as a preparation for reading Plato's *Sophist,* calls this a "peculiar etymological relation," one that he also finds in Plato's *Cratylus* (Martin Heidegger, *Plato's "Sophist,"* 36).

47. Plato, *The Dialogues of Plato,* trans. Benjamin Jowett (New York: Random House, 1937), 1:339–40 (216d).

48. Aristotle, *Nicomachean Ethics,* trans. Ross, 107–8. Plato equates *sōphrosunē* (translated as "temperance") with both wisdom and virtue as a whole in the *Protagoras* (*The Dialogues of Plato,* 1:103 [333]).

49. Aristotle, *Nicomachean Ethics,* trans. Terence Irwin (Indianapolis: Hackett, 1985), 428. This is also where Irwin takes issue with Aristotle's etymology for *sōphrosunē.*

50. Gilbert Murray, *Five Stages of Greek Religion* (Garden City, N.Y.: Doubleday, 1951), 188. I would like to thank my colleague *emeritus* Joseph Uemura for this reference and for his help with the complexities of Aristotle here, although I must add that he would probably disagree with the use I make of them.

51. Robert Bernasconi argues, on the basis of a preliminary text of Heidegger's *Plato's "Sophist,"* that the concept of "circumspection (*Umsicht*)" in *Being and Time* owes much to Aristotle's account of *phronēsis,* if not to *sōphrosunē* itself, and describes Heidegger's process as one of "destruction," or more precisely as "appropriation (*Aneignung*)" (Bernasconi, "Heidegger's Destruction of Phronesis," 140). He also explains that this "seeing around oneself" works for both authors in one way that seems very close to the concept of the appropriate as it has been delineated

and Difference, while addressing the propriety of the *propre,* Derrida notes something that would seem to be important "in truth beyond measure": "The unity of these significations, hidden beneath their apparent dispersion, the unity of the proper as the non-pollution of the subject absolutely close to himself, does not occur before the Latin era of philosophy (*proprius* is attached to proper)."[52] Again, Aristotle can still name a gift, a singular one, that is not *propre,* neither proper nor one's own, a gift that may be merely appropriate, just as he can still name a proportionality that is broader than justice as a distribution of goods, a moral excellence for which the economic virtue of justice can still be only one among others, and *dikē,* or a law beyond the law, more basic than the equity (*epieikēs,* "decency") that might more explicitly correspond to a legal concept of the appropriate in Aristotle.[53] Derrida is undoubtedly correct in linking to a time after Aristotle the chain that runs from *proprius* through the *propre* to the appropriate, and it is likely that the link between that chain and the one that includes appropriation and property (in the legal sense, at least) comes even later.[54] If so, the possibility would remain that we could look to the Aristotelian concepts of *sōphrosunē* and *phronēsis* as guides to what the appropriate might be outside or beyond the modern realm of property and appropriation.

2

I would argue that there is a certain arrogance in anachronistically insisting on the modern sense of words such as "appropriate," in Aris-

---

here: "For Aristotle it is not a rule but the situation itself which seems to make the demand on someone to act in a specific way. And that means that everything depends on one's ability to see the situation" (133). A similar reading of the relationship between Heidegger and Aristotle seems to be implied by Hans-Georg Gadamer in *Truth and Method,* 2d ed., trans. Joel Weinsheimer and Donald G. Marshall (New York: Crossroad Press, 1989), 312–24.

52. Jacques Derrida, *Writing and Difference,* trans. Alan Bass (Chicago: University of Chicago Press, 1978), 183.

53. See Aristotle, *Nicomachean Ethics,* trans. Ross, 132–34.

54. Hiroshi Matsuo of Yokohama National University suggests that the linking of personality, political/personal dominion, and justice can be traced to Grotius. He also makes an explicit contrast, which he finds in Grotius himself, between the latter's sense of justice, based on property, and Aristotle's concept of justice, based on the balancing of gains and losses. See Matsuo's "Historical and Theoretical Intimacy Between the Concepts of Rights and Property," *European Journal of Law,*

totle's sense of *sōphrosunē,* when dealing with premodern texts.⁵⁵ This may be especially so in the ethical realm, where Bernard Williams has cogently argued that our Kantian ideas deeply distort our understanding of the ancient Greek concepts.⁵⁶ His immediate reference here is to a concept of shame that seems closely tied to my discussion of the appropriate, and one that he also prefers as a moral guide over the "modern" concept of guilt (in terms of the Kantian moral law). Some of Williams's formulations even echo the arguments from the Madwoman's "trial" of the minions of modernity.⁵⁷ Moreover, his contrast between "modern" and ancient ways of thinking is based on the presence or absence of a faith in the ultimate "safety" or rationality of human existence, which resonates both with my nonfoundationalist starting point and with Giraudoux's famous play, *La Guerre de Troie n'aura pas lieu* (literally, "The Trojan War will not happen").⁵⁸ Not that Williams, Heidegger, or I believe we can return to the ancient Greek meanings of these concepts, but without some sense of them we cannot reach beyond the modern moral law. Indeed, some premodern sense of appropriateness may contaminate the modern meanings as much as it is contaminated by them—it may be, for example, that we do not perceive the invisible difference between appropriate and appropriate, that is, that we first see the undeclined verb as the adjective, "to appropriate" in terms of the appropriate.

A quite different approach to the problem of rethinking modern European philosophy by opening it to what is both external and, in some sense, internal to it—an approach with, I would argue, results similar to my own—can be found in the work of some of those currently working in African philosophy. The label "African philosophy" is somewhat misleading, of course, since the diversity of work in this area is enormous. Generally, however, the field is divided into three main streams of thought: ethnophilosophy, based on the specific traditions of the

---

Philosophy, and Computer Science 3 (1995) (*17th IVR World Congress—"Challenges to Law at the End of the 20th Century"*): 11–17.

55. My thinking about this issue has benefited from discussions with Iris Marion Young and Linda Nicholson.

56. Williams, *Shame and Necessity,* 77.

57. See, for example, Williams, *Shame and Necessity,* 94

58. Williams, *Shame and Necessity,* 164–66. Note that the usual English translation of Giraudoux's title is, as noted in the Preface, *Tiger at the Gates,* which obscures its concern with the limits of human rationality and action and its relationship to the Homeric texts, topics that are of primary interest to Williams.

many African cultures and linguistic groups; universalistic philosophy, which adapts the methods and concepts of European philosophers to the particular situation of Africa; and hermeneutics, which applies the work of Heidegger, Gadamer, and others to traditional and contemporary African practices and texts.[59] The two authors I discuss—Kwasi Wiredu, who would fall into the second group, and Tsenay Serequeberhan, who would fall into the third—also differ in national origin (Ghanaian/Akan and Ethiopian/Eritrean), politics (traditional liberal and nontraditional Marxist), as well as undoubtedly in other ways. At the same time, their projects seem to overlap each other and mine at least in attempting to understand traditional European philosophy from the perspective of " 'outside' voices with insights that they hope will radically transform the exclusionary mainstream canonical texts and narratives."[60]

Serequeberhan makes the rather strong claim that "African philosophy—even when its protagonists are not aware of it—is inherently, and cannot but be, a hermeneutic undertaking."[61] Deeply concerned with a political repudiation of neocolonialism, he is in the situation of having to do ethics, or something very much like it, on a strongly nonfoundational philosophical basis. He does not, however, seem to consider that task to be as problematic as has been suggested here: "[H]ermeneutical reflection opens to *praxis* the proper theoretical space to explore and suggest the normative alignment of its emancipatory projects and practical undertakings." In the case of African philosophy, this takes the specific form of determining "the 'justice' and 'justness' that originates out of the disappointed possibilities of our past, from whence we project a future." Thus, much of what he offers as an account of the hermeneutical bases of political action reads like the preceding description of how to determine appropriate action in the moral realm. "The struggle is not aimed at a certain 'stage' nor is it directed by or toward a given pre-established 'ideology.' Its only

---

59. For one source of this list, in addition to the two books discussed below, see Samuel Oluoch Imbo, "The Special Political Responsibilities of African Philosophers," *International Studies in Philosophy* 29, no. 1 (1997): 58.

60. Imbo, "Political Responsibilities of African Philosophers," 66. For more on this point, see also my *Is Women's Philosophy Possible?* (Savage, Md.: Rowman & Littlefield, 1990).

61. Tsenay Serequeberhan, *The Hermeneutics of African Philosophy: Horizon and Discourse* (New York: Routledge, 1994), 2.

theoretic concerns are the possibilities opened up by the struggle itself which are properly explored and articulated as its own grounded self-awareness."[62] He believes that by addressing African history and tradition in this way, a genuinely African philosophy can be developed, despite the origins of this method in Heidegger's rather culturally specific understanding of Greco-German thought.

Wiredu wants to rest his ethics and political thought in part on a distinction between morality, which he regards as universal because it encodes the conditions necessary for human social life, and customs, which he regards as responses to specific social and environmental conditions and hence, like language, particular to a certain culture. He seems to believe that the worst evils of colonial universalism might have been avoided if the Europeans had not taken their own (Christian) customs and forced them on others as vital moral truths.[63] Even in the case of morality proper, however, cross-cultural discussion of ethical principle must be grounded in a deep understanding of a specific tradition: "The assumption is not that truth necessarily resides in the speculative promptings of the African vernacular, but only that an indispensable preparation for cross-cultural evaluations of thought is conceptual clarity at both cultural ends." Thus, paradoxically, it is Wiredu, with his background in the analytic philosophy of language, who limits his discussion largely to the practices of his own Akan tradition, and the hermeneutically oriented Serequeberhan who speaks globally about neocolonial exploitation in Africa. While Wiredu's ethics relies on a roughly Kantian rule, which he calls "the principle of sympathetic impartiality," based on human needs, he adds in his postscript that he has limited himself to discussing the Akan tradition because "it cannot be taken for granted that all cultures have the same understanding of what it is to be human."[64]

We must act. All action manifests a rule. To seek to act without rules is to invite all the wrong rules into the arena, the more so the evil to be fought is global, ancient, and calls itself by the name of law or God. What rule, then, best suits a feminism, or an African philosophy, aimed

---

62. Serequeberhan, *Hermeneutics of African Philosophy*, 27, 29, and 110.
63. Kwasi Wiredu, *Cultural Universals and Particulars: An African Perspective* (Bloomington: Indiana University Press, 1996), 2.
64. Wiredu, *Cultural Universals and Particulars*, 118, 29, and 201.

at combating oppression of all kinds? Perhaps a rule, or nonrule, of appropriate action could provide us with both a guide to moral choice and a vantage point that could allow for critical ethical evaluation without requiring a supposedly universal metaphysics. If such a concept of appropriate behavior can be separated from the history that ties it, in the modern era, to the proper, property, and appropriation, but nevertheless can retain full awareness of the impossibility of a total separation, then the concept of the appropriate might indicate one way we may be able to satisfy both our desire for a critical morality and our need to acknowledge the irretrievable loss of any metaphysical foundation for ethical thought. The bare possibility of such an impossible reappropriation of a rule of appropriate action, morality without rules, is hinted at by Derrida in *On the Name:* "What is the ethicity of ethics? The morality of morality? What is responsibility? . . . These questions are always urgent. In a certain way they must remain urgent and unanswered, at any rate without a general and rule-governed response, without a response other than that which is linked specifically each time, to the occurrence of a decision without rules and without will in the course of a new test of the undecidable."[65]

---

65. Jacques Derrida, *On the Name,* ed. Thomas Dutoit (Stanford: Stanford University Press, 1995), 16–17.

2
The Appropriate Past

> Every founding and even every appearance of foundability has inevitably degraded being into some sort of a being. Being *qua* being remains groundless.
> —Martin Heidegger, *The Principle of Reason*

Teaching is learning. When I began to teach ethics, I was surprised to learn that my students found Plato's *Gorgias* easier to understand than Aristotle's *Nicomachean Ethics*. I thought for a while that the difference was the ease with which the Plato could be reduced to the slogan "It is better to suffer unjust actions than to do them," whereas Aristotle offered no such shortcuts. In time, however, I noticed that the reverse situation held with regard to Kant and Mill: while Kant's categorical imperative is more easily reduced to a slogan than Mill's utilitarianism, that fact seemed to make it no easier for my students to understand his moral reasoning, whereas they had little problem with Mill. A chance conversation with an especially articulate student finally made it clear what was really going on. My undergraduates read Plato as if he were espousing Christian mind(soul)/body dualism. They made sense of his work in terms of the sermons many of them had heard all their lives about valuing the things of the soul, or spirit, above those of the body. Somewhat more accurately, they were understanding Mill in terms of what they were learning in their biology and psychology courses, that is, as an ethical theory based on the assumption that humans were merely complex animals. In the cases of Aristotle and Kant, on the other hand, they had no preexisting model of the human to provide the foundation for the ethical theories they were learning. Thus, while to the trained eye Kantian and Aristotelian ethics are extremely different, to my students they were alike in the incomprehensibility of their theories, and both were in stark contrast to the (seeming) clarity of Plato and Mill.

The first lesson that I drew from this revelation was that ethics cannot so easily be separated from metaphysics as the current way of dividing up the philosophy curriculum (and, indeed, the profession) might suggest. A corollary lesson was that the way in which my students were understanding the complex material in front of them made perfect sense. If human beings have potentially separable physical and spiritual components, and especially if only the spiritual component is immortal, then clearly we should value that part of ourselves above all else and act accordingly. There is, after all, a certain symmetry between the lives of Socrates and Jesus that Kierkegaard, for instance, makes full use of in his philosophical work. Whether this is an entirely accurate understanding of Plato's philosophy or whether it requires an omnipotent, omniscient, infinitely good Creator may make relatively little difference to the moral implications that might be drawn from this position, which are, after all, the primary concern of students in an introductory ethics course. A similar argument would suggest that, if humans are merely complex animals, then what motivates other animals, that is, pleasure, is the only possible basis for human morality. In contrast, Kant and Aristotle are just too unlike anything else in my students' intellectual universe for them to make sense of their philosophies at all, a problem they tended to blame on the difficulty of the writing, rather than the difficulty of the ideas involved. (Plato is similarly alien, of course, but gives the appearance of being translatable into something familiar.)

That lesson learned, in teaching the ethics of Aristotle and Kant, I devoted considerably more time and effort to explaining what the two philosophers considered to be characteristic of the human. In so doing, I discovered another wisdom in my students' "ignorance": both thinkers have what might be called an ethics of aspiration, as contrasted to the "ethics of description" found in Mill and (to my students' eyes) in

Plato. Aristotle expects humans to want to be as fully human as possible, where that is a state to be achieved, not a mere given of one's biological genus. That is why at least some men can be motivated to contemplation as their life's goal, despite its obvious material drawbacks. Indeed, in that case the aspiration is to be more than human, godlike, a goal incomprehensible in itself to contemporary post-Christian culture. Kant is also not content to take us as we are, but believes that we can be drawn by the idea of pure duty to act beyond any possible limit of self-interest, even presumably beyond the long-term self-interest of our immortal souls. Pure duty is its own, its only justification, unless we are to fall back into religious heteronomy. I expended considerable effort in trying to instill a sense of the grandeur of both views of human possibility into my students, with little clear improvement in their understanding of either Aristotle or Kant. Second lesson: teaching is not preaching. Second corollary: explaining the obscure by the more obscure doesn't work, especially if the latter is as obscure as Aristotelian or Kantian metaphysics.

Not that the changes in my teaching were completely without effect, they just didn't have the effect I wanted, that is, a more accurate understanding of Aristotle's and Kant's ethical work. What happened instead was that at least some of my students learned a different "wrong" version of their ideas. Seeing the relevance of metaphysics to ethics, they attached what metaphysics they did understand to these two ethical systems. It soon became clear that what I could most reasonably expect was Kant retranslated back into traditional Christianity, so that we are impelled to do our duty by the fear of God and the noumenal self becomes the immortal soul. The analogy between humans and other natural kinds, so clear to my students when we discussed Mill, escaped them entirely when put in Aristotelian terms, so that the only way that they could bring metaphysics to bear on his ethics transformed him into a quasi-nihilistic relativist involved in an empirical account of the conventional moral system of the Attic Greeks. Thus I was left with two more serious misunderstandings to go with the apparently irreducible distortion of Plato's work that I had first discovered. Not a clear improvement, by anyone's standards. Strangely, however, now that these students thought they understood the metaphysical bases of Aristotle's and Kant's ethics, they actually did a better job of applying them to concrete cases; that is, in one dimension they *did* understand them better.

Third lesson: Aristotelian and Kantian ethics seem to be in some sense severable from their supposed metaphysical foundations. Third corollary: this should come as no surprise, given the many Christian interpretations of both ethical systems. That these ethics are thus compatible with such a radically different set of metaphysical assumptions gives some *prima facie* credence to the claim that they are not logically tied to the metaphysics from which they arose. Careful study of the relevant texts by these authors, and by their major contemporary interpreters, reveals the clear possibility of such a failure of logical entailment in both cases and indicates, moreover, that both philosophers may have been aware of this problem. Final lesson: these two foundational texts of Western metaphysics deconstruct themselves along a line that threatens one of the most basic foundational beliefs, that ethics is logically dependent on metaphysics. In what follows, I argue for a somewhat stronger position, that the link between ethics and metaphysics in Kant and Aristotle is not foundational, but rather arises from the fact that their ethical systems are based on a rationalized concept of appropriate action, where the nature of reason (and so metaphysics) serves to guide the process of rationalization, but provides no absolute foundation. Final corollary: while the Madwoman is not concerned with either virtue or duty, that is, while her decision is not fully rationalized in these ways (and cannot be, given the nature of Giraudoux's polemic against modernity), her reason might rely in some nonlogical way on a sense of the appropriate, just as in Aristotle and Kant.

True Foundations

What would constitute a relation of entailment between a set of metaphysical assumptions and an ethics? Such a relationship was sketched out above with regard to my students' misunderstanding of Plato and Mill. Here I would like to provide a more detailed outline of a strong relationship between metaphysics and ethics, as indicated in Plato's *Gorgias* and Mill's *Utilitarianism,* with a view to the contrast between this relationship and what I believe to be the much looser one found in Aristotle and Kant. That is, I suggest that the metaphysical commitments apparent in both Plato and Mill determine specific concepts of the human, although very different ones in each case.[1] These concepts of what human existence is then directly entail the respective moral rules developed by these two philosophers. There is little in either of these ethical systems that would correspond to the concept of appropriate action I am using here, because each has a fixed and determinate end state for human life—knowledge of the Good or the greatest happiness for the greatest number—in terms of which individual actions can be specified and judged. My claim about Aristotle and Kant is that their metaphysical systems do not entail such a determinate goal for human action and hence that their ethical systems are neither justified in the same foundational way as those of Plato and Mill nor capable of providing similar rules for human conduct.

Before beginning with Plato and Mill, however, it might be advisable to address the peculiar combination of thinkers that my avowedly inaccurate starting point has generated. Whatever my students may think, Plato and Mill are probably the least similar of these four thinkers. Despite the fact that Mill insists that Socrates was a utilitarian,[2] his own basic assumptions about human nature and the goal of human life are very similar to those of Socrates' opponents in *Gorgias*. The primary difference is that Mill has a more subtle concept of pleasure and a broader view of how to achieve it than do Callicles and his cohorts. As Nietzsche suggests, utilitarianism can be seen as the democratic form of Greek aristocratic hedonism, Callicles without the nobility.[3] The other three thinkers in question here, by contrast, share a concern with the noble, with duty, that seems to transcend the calculation of long-term benefit. But that, the tradition tells us, is because they share a mind(spirit)/body dualism that Mill apparently lacks, a dualism that logically entails different ethical conclusions. While there is a crucial dualism in Plato, although not the one my students think, I argue that dualism so conceived may well be lacking in Aristotle, and may serve a very different purpose in Kant. Thus the relationship

---

1. At the urging of my colleague Duane Cady, I must say at this point that it is not, strictly speaking, the philosophy of Plato that is in question here so much as the traditional understanding of that philosophy, perhaps better termed "Platonism." That is why this discussion is specifically limited to *Gorgias* and, to a lesser extent, the *Republic*, which hew closer to the traditional "Platonist" line than others of his dialogues.
2. See Mill's *Utilitarianism,* ed. George Sher (Indianapolis: Hackett, 1979), 1.
3. On this, see, for instance, Friedrich Nietzsche, *The Portable Nietzsche,* trans. and ed. Walter Kaufmann (New York: Viking, 1968), 444–46.

between metaphysics (dualistic or not) and ethics is different in these latter two thinkers.

1

How does one derive the conclusion that "it is better to suffer unjust actions than to do them"? In three ways, which may explain my students' (and perhaps Mill's) misreading of Plato's text. My students focus on the argument that comes toward the end of *Gorgias* (523–27),[4] where Socrates tells about the judgment of the dead. This tale is expressed explicitly in terms of the separation of (what gets translated as) body and soul (524b), and links evil or unjust actions to visible scars on the soul that mark the dead as unworthy of the Isles of the Blessed, that is, as damned (525a). As I suggested above, the ethical implications of the (easily Christianized) metaphysics of this story are clear. A second sort of argument occurs roughly in the middle of Socrates' dialogue with Callicles (491d–508c). There the dispute is put in terms of a disciplined or a self-indulgent life, rather than in terms of suffering or doing unjust actions, but the basic point remains the same because self-discipline is what allows us to suffer unjust actions without doing them, and what shows us the necessity of doing so (508c). By focusing on discipline here, however, Plato invites another sort of misinterpretation, the one compatible with Mill's moral theory (and perhaps, to some extent, Aristotle's). If the argument against self-indulgence is that one can better maximize pleasure by controlling one's desire, by choosing the "better" over the "worse" pleasures (500a), by acting "appropriately" or "properly" (507a–b), and perhaps by avoiding doing unjust acts and suffering them nobly, then we seem to be squarely in the utilitarian realm.

There are good reasons, however, for thinking that neither of these is Plato's favored account of why "doing what's unjust is more to be guarded against than suffering it" (527b). One such reason is the various symmetries between the argument of *Gorgias* and that of the *Republic:* the topics of conversation are much the same in both cases; Callicles makes many of the same claims as Thrasymachus; the earlier

---

4. Plato, *Gorgias,* trans. Donald J. Zeyl (Indianapolis: Hackett, 1987), 107–13. Hereafter references to this text will be made by marginal page numbers in parentheses.

dispute with Polus has analogies with the initial debates of the *Republic;* and the relationships of reality and illusion in that work are reflected in the various forms of "pandering" found in *Gorgias.* Drawing on this symmetry between the two dialogues, one can develop an argument that seems more in tune with the total structure of Plato's thought (or at least with the dominant interpretation of it). This argument does require a division of body and "soul" (464a), but without relying on the afterlife to validate its conclusion. Rather, it relies on the subordination of the body to the soul and the analogy between the corresponding crafts that serve them: "[W]hat cosmetics is to gymnastics, sophistry is to legislation, and what pastry baking is to medicine, oratory is to justice" (465c). The argument, then, is that just as medicine is to be preferred to all else in the care and repair of the body, so justice is to be preferred to all else in the care and repair of the soul. This not because of some long-term benefit in terms of pleasure/pain or salvation/damnation, but because knowledge of what is real and true is intrinsically good and what brings about such knowledge in the self (justice) or others (legislation) is, like health, also intrinsically good.

The intrinsic worth of knowledge reappears several times in this dialogue, both to subordinate ethics to knowledge and to disallow the two misinterpretations just noted. Knowledge is necessary, first of all, to the proper management of pleasures, so that one will do what one wants (the true Good), rather than merely what one sees fit (the apparent good) (466d–468e). Knowledge is also needed to tell the better from the worse pleasures (500a). Utilitarianism is not a full account of the good life, as Aristotle acknowledges,[5] because it ignores how knowledge determines even the role of pleasure in one's life. Furthermore, it is devotion to truth, not following moral rules per se, that marks the soul of the good man in the afterlife. Legislation is subordinate to private morality because it must be played out in the public realm, with all its dangers of corruption (526a–c). It is this last point that supports Socrates over Callicles: the political life has no worth except as an arena for practicing justice, which might for all that best be carried out in private. To borrow the language of the *Republic:* knowledge of the transcendental Good is paramount in life; all other possible goods (and

---

5. On this, see J. L. Austin's "*Agathon* and *Eudaimonia* in the *Ethics* of Aristotle," in *Philosophical Papers* (New York: Oxford University Press, 1970), 1–31.

all other realities) flow from that; and so whatever might interfere with such knowledge, the illusions of the body or of public honor, would be the greatest evil. Therefore, it is always better to suffer unjust acts than to do them, and the best life is that of the philosopher, who not only seems to be good but is good. The pivotal metaphysical claim here is not mind/body dualism, but the dualism between reality and appearance, from which all the ethical conclusions follow.

2

The distinguishing difference, then, between Plato's ethics and Mill's would be less the absence of dualism in Mill than the absence of that particular dualism. While I believe that my students are less wrong in attributing a certain materialism, or perhaps biologism, to Mill's views in *Utilitarianism* than they are with regard to Plato's dualism, it is also possible to focus on what would be one of the main implications of any such materialism in Mill, the absence of a clear demarcation between reality and appearance. (This would be a common feature of all philosophy in the empiricist tradition, including Berkeley's immaterialism, as Descartes argued against Hobbes and Hume affirmed with a certain perverse delight.)[6] This is most clearly shown in Mill's central argument, that what is desired must be what is desirable. Since pleasure, broadly construed, is what humans desire, it follows that pleasure must be the good, the goal of human action.[7] Not only is there no recognition here of the difference between what is and what ought to be the case (an error that subsequent Anglo-American ethical thought attempted to correct under the heading of the "naturalistic fallacy"), but more important for my purposes, there is no recognition of the possibility of mistaking the apparent good for the real good of human action. What seems to be good must be good, except insofar as what gives us pleasure has been perverted. Even in the case of perversion,

---

6. On Hobbes, see René Descartes, *The Philosophical Works of Descartes*, trans. Elizabeth S. Haldane and G.R.T. Ross (New York: Cambridge University Press, 1931), 2:78. (This reference is to "an Atheist," but Descartes makes it clear that he regards Hobbes's materialism as tantamount to atheism.) For Hume, see, for example, David Hume, *An Enquiry Concerning Human Understanding*, ed. Eric Steinberg (Indianapolis: Hackett, 1977), 105.
7. Mill, *Utilitarianism*, 34.

moreover, there must be some real good hidden in the apparent one, as a true understanding of the instrumental value of money for obtaining pleasure is hidden in the perverted priorities of the miser.[8]

This "proof" of the utilitarian principle comes in chapter 4 of the book, after Mill has made certain that pleasure will be broadly construed, and has argued the close tie between what utilitarianism demands in the moral realm and what humans, insofar as they are social animals, are naturally inclined to do. This last point reinforces the parallels between human and animal behavior that underlie the entire argument. In chapter 2, Mill has already suggested that human pleasures are different from those of animals not in kind, as Aristotle's tripartite soul would suggest, but in their use of our more developed mental abilities: "Human beings have faculties more elevated than the animal appetites and, when once made conscious of them, do not regard anything as happiness which does not include their gratification."[9] Again, that we take it to be so is counted as evidence that it is so, that the "animal" pleasures are indeed inferior to the intellectual ones. In spite of the fact that the more elevated pleasures, and greater intellectual awareness in general, can bring more pains in their wake, the subjective human preference for greater, rather than less, awareness proves its true greater value. "What is there to decide whether a particular pleasure is worth purchasing at the cost of a particular pain," Mill argues, "except the feelings and judgments of the experienced."[10] The judgments of the experienced, note, not of those who have knowledge. By such measure, Callicles may be imprudent or perverse in his claims and judgments, but he is not wrong in the way in which Socrates' knowledge of the true Good allows him to be certain Callicles is wrong.

If the only correction for the illusions of bodily experience is further bodily experience, that is, if empiricism is true, then the only corrective for moral illusions such as Callicles' choice of unlimited bodily pleasure is an argument that would pit short-term pleasures against long-term ones and "worse" pleasures that rely on a prior pain against "better" ones that do not, as Socrates does in the middle section of *Gorgias,* or animalistic pleasures against more intellectual ones and "perverse"

---

8. Mill, *Utilitarianism,* 36.
9. Mill, *Utilitarianism,* 8.
10. Mill, *Utilitarianism,* 11.

pleasures against the ones more "natural" to humans as social beings, as Mill does. Mill gives, however, no further argument that short-term, "worse," perverse, and animalistic pleasures are only apparent goods, in contrast to some real Good. On the contrary, he clearly considers them to be real pleasures and to that extent real, if limited, goods, at least to those for whom they are pleasures. In the final chapter of *Utilitarianism* he argues that the remaining demarcation between appearance and reality in the moral realm, the concept of justice as overriding utilitarian concerns, is in fact derived from the utilitarian principle itself[11] and so ultimately from what is (apparently) the case, not from some abstract or transcendent knowledge of what must (really) be the case. Mill does not want to teach us about the Good, but about the correct understanding of pleasure and its role in moral life. Given the empiricist assumptions on which he relies, even without an explicit metaphysical commitment to materialism and the corresponding analogy between animal and human goods, this is the only logical way he can lead us to the good life, to justice and ethics in the fullest sense.

Both Plato and Mill *can* lead us to the good life, can give us clear rules about how to get there, because both have a fully determinate idea of what the good life is. That idea, in turn, derives from their understanding of what human beings are: for Plato, our essential existence is as souls capable of aspiring to the Good, which severely limits the role of pleasure in the properly lived human life; for Mill, we are primarily animals, motivated by pleasures as animals are, with no access to any external, transcendent reality from which critically to examine whether pleasure itself is a good. These are opposite views, yet the same, at least when taken in opposition to the possibility or the necessity of nonfoundational ethics, where the lack of metaphysical certainties of any kind (even biologistic, scientistic, or materialistic ones) leaves no determinate goal for human life and only a more or less rationalized concept of appropriate action to provide limits for our personal or collective moral beliefs—when taken in opposition, that is, to the ethics of Aristotle and Kant.

---

11. Mill, *Utilitarianism*, 63.

The Appropriate Virtue

To state my point about Platonism somewhat differently, it could be said that his ethics relies on the existence of a transcendental reality that provides the forms for our empirical existence. Knowledge of the transcendental form of the Good, in particular, provides the rules needed for the rational part of the human soul to steer the irrational, appetitive parts to a truly virtuous life, as a driver would control the horses drawing his chariot.[12] Metaphysics and ethics here are woven into a seamless cloth, whatever our conclusions about the status of the resulting picture. Aristotle, of course, also believes that beings are what they are because of the form that supplies their essence, but these forms are immanent to reality, not transcendent to it. For him, morality consists, not in the control of the appetitive soul, but in a proper balance between our correct and necessary desires and our reason. The goal is not to eliminate anger, but to channel it to "the right person, to the right extent, at the right time, with the right motive, and in the right way" (1109a).[13] The ethical question, then, is how to determine the principle that would guide this balance. The traditional answer to that question, based on the model provided by Plato, is that the metaphysical form of human being, that is, that we are rational animals, logically determines the ethical conclusions that Aristotle draws. That is apparently Aristotle's own view, or at least his goal, although, as was said above, it cannot be the view of anyone who would wish to incorporate his ethical thought into a Christian tradition that defines humans in terms of immortal soul and sinful body.

I have already indicated that one reason for the basic incompatibility between Aristotle's metaphysics and Christian doctrine is that Aristotle is not the right sort of dualist, as opposed, arguably, to Plato. There is in Aristotle a difference between form and matter that corresponds in some way to the difference between mind and body, but they are not clearly separable or clearly in conflict in their desires. For Aristotle, the most important aspects of ethical life, like the forms, are

---

12. See Plato, *The Dialogues of Plato,* trans. Benjamin Jowett (New York: Random House, 1937), 1:250–51 (246).

13. Aristotle, *Nicomachean Ethics,* trans. David Ross (New York: Oxford University Press, 1980), 45. Hereafter references to this text will be made by marginal page numbers in parentheses.

immanent, that is, social and political, not transcendent or spiritual. As Bernard Williams puts it with regard to early Christian views of slavery, "[T]hey invoke a dualism, or some similar picture of human beings, by which the most essential characteristics and interests of people transcend the empirical social world and its misfortunes. Aristotle did not have such a picture."[14] One main concern of contemporary commentaries on Aristotle, especially on his ethics, is to warn us against reading him in modern terms, and specifically in terms of post-Cartesian epistemological and metaphysical preoccupations. Even Heidegger comments on his status as preeminently premodern: "Aristotle was the last of the great philosophers who had eyes to see and, what is still more decisive, the energy and the tenacity to continue to force inquiry back to the phenomena and to the seen and to mistrust from the ground up all wild and windy speculation, no matter how close to the heart of common sense."[15]

1

The determining feature of Aristotle's metaphysics lies in his concept of the essence of something, what makes a thing the thing that it is, its "primary being."[16] In book 7 of the *Metaphysics,* he cites four candidates for such primary being: the form of the thing (as opposed to the matter), the universal through which it is understood (as opposed to its particularity), the genus that defines it (as opposed to

14. Bernard Williams, *Shame and Necessity* (Berkeley and Los Angeles: University of California Press, 1993), 116.
15. Martin Heidegger, *The Basic Problems of Phenomenology,* trans. Albert Hofstadter (Bloomington: Indiana University Press, 1982), 232.
16. Unlike my understanding of the other philosophers discussed in depth here, my understanding of Aristotle's work is severely limited by a lack of the necessary specialized training, most especially by my inability to read Greek. In addition to relying on comments on my work made by my colleague Duane Cady, who does have the requisite background, the following discussion draws heavily on what are generally taken to be two of the best current commentaries on Aristotle's work, a general account of the structure of his metaphysical and ethical arguments by Terence Irwin, *Aristotle's First Principles* (New York: Cambridge University Press, 1988), and a more specific study of his ethics by Sarah Broadie, *Ethics with Aristotle* (New York: Oxford University Press, 1991). It is important to remember, however, that both these authors have projects of their own with regard to Aristotle, neither of which corresponds to my project here. At the same time, they both develop, for their own purposes, an account of how Aristotle's metaphysics and ethics can be understood to come apart.

its species), and its status as subject or substance (*hypokeimenon,* as opposed to its attributes or accidents).[17] It is in this context that his concept of form, *eidos,* can be determined to be immanent because of its necessary manifestation in matter,[18] but the other considerations indicate that form is not to be taken in an overly literal sense. The "form" of human beings is not their bipedal mammality, but the universal through which they are understood in a primary way, their defining characteristic, that is, their rationality. Whatever other attributes humans may have, this is what remains central to their being what they are. Birds are also bipedal, but in a way that is less defining of them than their ability to fly. This is because primary being functions causally in natural kinds, for Aristotle, as both formal and final cause.[19] That is, the form for birds must involve flight because that is the purpose, or the goal, of being a bird. Feathers, wings, and consequently bipedalism are attributes that follow from that purpose, not defining characteristics that explain it. Similarly, human bipedalism is the result, not the cause, of human rationality (or, if the cause in an evolutionary sense, only an efficient, not a final, cause).

Thus, the linchpin that connects Aristotle's metaphysics and his ethics can be found in his derivation of the final *telos,* or Good, for humans. To do this, he ties human purpose to human function: "[F]or all things that have a function or activity, the good and the 'well' is thought to reside in the function, so would it seem to be for man, if he has a function" (*Nicomachean Ethics* 1097b). The function of man resides in his "primary being" as a rational animal, where rationality refers to both the rational soul itself and that part of the appetitive soul that follows the dictates of reason. Thus, "human good turns out to be activity of the soul exhibiting excellence [virtue, *arete*]" (1098a). The two implicit contrasts here are with Platonism, in which it was only the purely rational soul that was concerned with the Good, and Eudoxus (and perhaps Mill), for whom pleasure was the good, regardless of the role of reason or activity. Still, Aristotle's purpose is constructive, not critical. He wants to know how to move from the foundation he has provided himself in the *Metaphysics* to the moral and political conclu-

17. Aristotle, *Metaphysics,* trans. Richard Hope (Ann Arbor: University of Michigan Press, 1960), 132. (My understanding of this passage owes a great deal to Sarah Broadie, *Ethics with Aristotle,* 416.)
18. Aristotle, *Metaphysics,* 149.
19. Irwin, *Aristotle's First Principles,* 246.

sions he and his audience already feel constitute the good life. The essence of human existence, and the life of intellectual excellence and moral virtue he believes it entails, provide the necessary connection. This reliance on human essence, however, opens his argument to empirical verification, or falsification, and thus to the realms of both common sense and psychology in a way that has no direct parallel in his discussion of the essences of material substances or nonhuman animals, where there is no internal intermediary between essence and actual behavior.

In Terence Irwin's terminology, this would be a case of "strong" dialectic, a dialectic that starts, not from what is generally taken to be the case, but from what must *be* the case.[20] "If common beliefs can be explained, and partly revised, by appeal to an account of human nature and the human soul, and the account in turn is defensible from first philosophy, then the conclusion of dialectical argument about ethics may claim some support outside the particular ethical common beliefs that are the starting point of the argument."[21] Irwin makes this claim because he believes that "pure" (Platonic) dialectic is not sufficient to make the link that Aristotle wants to make between his metaphysics and his ethics.[22] It must be remembered here, however, that the concept of "strong" dialectic is part of Irwin's re-creation, not part of Aristotle's argument: "Aristotle does not say that his crucial premisses derive support from strong dialectic and from first philosophy. But I argue that in fact this support is available."[23] While this is not the place to argue the plausibility of Irwin's re-creation of Aristotle, it is well worth noting that Irwin himself thinks that, in its absence, the link that Aristotle believes he has made between human essence and human good is not clearly established, or at least not beyond the level of "pure" dialectic, which Irwin believes can provide only coherence as a criterion of truth and thus falls short of giving objective principles.[24]

While one could simply deny that rationality is the essence of human life by asserting that language and reason are coincident properties of what is basically a highly complex animal existence (as Mill might believe), that approach would also ignore the relationship between

20. Irwin, *Aristotle's First Principles*, 176–77
21. Irwin, *Aristotle's First Principles*, 24.
22. See, for instance, Irwin, *Aristotle's First Principles*, 365, 449, and 468.
23. Irwin, *Aristotle's First Principles*, 475.
24. Irwin, *Aristotle's First Principles*, 478 and 482.

essence and final cause in Aristotle, a thoroughly modern move that I would hope to avoid here. Even in Aristotle's own terms, however, we could ask about the role of empirical considerations in determining essence or primary being. Is it really self-evident that flying *is* the essential nature of birds? Does flying have no purpose beyond itself? Is the measure of a bird's worth its excellence at flying? Are penguins and ostriches defective birds? Similarly, one can ask whether rationality is either the essential nature or the ultimate end of human life. Why not pleasure? Because, Aristotle says, all animals experience pleasure, so it cannot be essential to us as human. But what if there were other rational beings?[25] Bats also fly. If there were rational, language-using four-legged (or finned) mammals, would bipedalism be part of our essence, as feathers are for birds? At the other extreme, how would Aristotle rule out the possibility that the primary being of human life is as the creature of an infinitely powerful, infinitely good divine Creator? Our understanding of the essence of mealworms is quite different if we see them as the larval stage of certain species of beetles, so why not our understanding of the essence of humans if they are seen as elements of a larger divine plan, rather than as containing within themselves their own ultimate purpose in life.[26]

Sarah Broadie's concern in *Ethics with Aristotle* is to refute misinterpretations of Aristotle's work by carefully reexamining and clarifying Aristotle's ethical arguments. One way she does this is to emphasize the extent to which his starting points, such as the essential rationality of human beings, already rely on ethical considerations, making the ethics, if not circular, at least a "pure" dialectic in Irwin's terms.[27] Broadie regards such a starting point in common belief as necessary to any plausible investigation in ethics, but clearly the relationship between metaphysics and any such investigation cannot be a strictly logical one. As already suggested, the metaphysics tells us that humans have an essence, not what that essence must be. When discussing happiness in Aristotle, Broadie points out that "[t]here seems

---

25. Broadie raises this possibility as part of her argument, discussed below, that rationality in Aristotle already serves as a normative criterion, not a descriptive one (*Ethics with Aristotle*, 35).
26. Broadie also raises this possibility with regard to the effect of such a difference in perspective on the role of pleasure in the ethical realm (*Ethics with Aristotle*, 352).
27. Broadie, *Ethics with Aristotle*, 35.

little chance of finding an independent or neutral theory of human nature on which to ground it."[28] This is central to Broadie's point because, if the ethics were logically dependent on the metaphysics, the subsequent refutation of the metaphysics would also have been a refutation of the ethics. The logical gap between the two is what allows Aristotelian ethics to remain relevant in a world in which Aristotelian metaphysics apparently no longer has a place.[29] Irwin believes Aristotle's arguments must be altered to meet modern skeptical objections, but Broadie reminds us that his ethics were not developed in response to modern problems of moral justification.[30] Rather than reformulate his arguments, as Irwin does, she seeks to make them clearer in order to validate them to a modern audience in Aristotle's own terms.

What Irwin and Broadie share is the sense that, despite Aristotle's aspirations, but consistent with his constant commitment to questioning his own most basic assumptions,[31] his metaphysical claims alone do not directly entail his ethical system. This is shown, according to Irwin's negative argument, by the inability of "pure" dialectic to move beyond the confines of common ethical beliefs to true objectivity and, according to Broadie, by the fact that other metaphysical systems such as Christianity are in theory compatible with Aristotle's ethical method. A different "function" for human life will yield different virtues, different visions of the good life. Alternatively, Aristotle's account of the good life might be compatible with other metaphysical beliefs, although, as Broadie suggests, in such contexts that account might lose some of Aristotle's unique moral spirit.[32] (One candidate for such an alternative metaphysical basis might be a secularized and less puritanical Kantian view, as Irwin sometimes seems to suggest.)[33] Thus, it seems at least arguable that Aristotle's ethics are nonfoundational in the sense used here, that is, that his metaphysical commitments do not entail a kind of transcendent moral truth in the same way the

---

28. Broadie, *Ethics with Aristotle*, 42. Note that Broadie cites Irwin as agreeing with her on this point (121 n. 35).
29. Broadie, *Ethics with Aristotle*, 157. Heidegger seems to want to argue that this supposed "refutation" is based on a major misunderstanding of Aristotle's metaphysics, for instance, in *Aristotle's "Metaphysics" Theta 1-3*, trans. Walter Brogan and Peter Warnek (Bloomington: Indiana University Press, 1995).
30. Broadie, *Ethics with Aristotle*, 219.
31. See Broadie, *Ethics with Aristotle*, 18.
32. Broadie, *Ethics with Aristotle*, 50.
33. See, for example, Irwin, *Aristotle's First Principles*, 360–61.

Good entails the moral dictates of Platonism. Hans-Georg Gadamer makes a stronger claim: "Aristotle became the founder of ethics as a discipline independent of metaphysics."[34]

2

Where, then, do Aristotle's ethical conclusions come from? Are they merely "pure" dialectical conclusions intent on justifying the moral standards of a particular time and place? That is the status Irwin accords some of Aristotle's more offensive moral and political beliefs, using the empirical element in their derivation to separate them from those conclusions he considers to be based on "strong" dialectic, which conveniently are the ones with which he (and I) might be more comfortable.[35] As suggested earlier, the reinterpretation of this point that I would like to argue in the present context is that Aristotle's ethics constitute an account of appropriate action in which dialectic (of whatever sort) is used to rationalize the concept of the appropriate so that, while falling short of actual moral rules, it can be understood and taught in terms of shared values that can both endorse common moral beliefs and also provide a critical basis for reevaluating those beliefs when they become problematic. As Broadie puts it, "We see from this that the ungeneralisability of the *orthos logos* [right reason or right principle] into a rule does not entail that it cannot be articulated by means of statements employing general terms. It is a *logos*, after all. What cannot be relied upon to hold good beyond the present case is its *orthotes*, its correctness."[36] Unlike Plato or Mill, Aristotle will not give us moral rules, or any way to derive them, but will help us learn how to determine what is the appropriate action in a given moral situation.

While it is difficult to trace any one word in Aristotle's text as fully equivalent to "appropriate" in the sense I am using it here, it is also difficult not to see the concept of appropriate action in many of his formulations. That would certainly be the most reasonable way to understand his repeated use of forms such as "The man, then, who faces and who fears the right things and from the right motive, in the right

---

34. Hans-Georg Gadamer, *Truth and Method,* 2d ed., trans. Joel Weinsheimer and Donald G. Marshall (New York: Crossroad Press, 1989), 312.
35. See, for example, Irwin, *Aristotle's First Principles,* 462.
36. Broadie, *Ethics with Aristotle,* 76.

way and at the right time, and who feels confident under the corresponding conditions, is brave" (*Nicomachean Ethics* 1115b). In any case, commentators on Aristotle find it hard to avoid the word "appropriate." Broadie defines the noble, or fine, as "connected with what is fitting, appropriate or in the broad sense just,"[37] and equates the appropriate response with the median response, or mean.[38] Nancy Sherman, in *The Fabric of Character*, similarly says that "[t]o hit the mean is to act in a way that is appropriate to the case," and defines the virtuous person for Aristotle as "one who knows how to act and feel in ways appropriate (*hos dei*) to the circumstances."[39] The word "appropriate" is needed here precisely because of the absence of moral rules, that is, the lack of a metaphysical foundation for his claims about a determinate end of all human action. The very fact that Aristotle relies so heavily on such formulations, as well as his explicit rejection of the possibility of deductive moral knowledge on the Platonic model (1049b), may well indicate that he was fully aware of the extent to which his "pure" dialectic failed to provide such a foundation.

Also, in relationship to the larger argument I am making here, it is worth noting that *sophrosune* (usually translated as "temperance" but also, as suggested in Chapter 1, a possible principle of appropriate action), while regarded as a minor or minimal moral virtue by Irwin, plays a much more central role in the other two commentaries. Sherman redefines *sophrosune,* much as Irwin himself does in the notes to his translation of the *Nicomachean Ethics*, as what preserves "reason or soundness of mind," a term used "to convey an overall sense of self."[40] Later she equates mature virtuous character with "the truly temperate person," or *sophron*.[41] Similarly, Broadie sees temperance as the point of coordination between the moral virtues and practical wisdom, citing Aristotle's claim that "without temperance one cannot be wise."[42] The *sophron,* the temperate person, is the one whose carefully developed sense of appropriate action within a particular cultural

37. Broadie, *Ethics with Aristotle*, 92.
38. Broadie, *Ethics with Aristotle*, 99.
39. Nancy Sherman, *The Fabric of Character* (New York: Oxford University Press, 1989), 49–50. Note that she cites Irwin here as agreeing with her characterization of Aristotle's view (51 n. 65).
40. Sherman, *The Fabric of Character*, 107. The Irwin reference is to *Nicomachean Ethics*, trans. Terence Irwin (Indianapolis: Hackett, 1985), 428.
41. Sherman, *The Fabric of Character*, 167.
42. Broadie, *Ethics with Aristotle*, 205.

context can be relied upon as the basis for more critical, dialectical evaluation of concrete social practices. Such a foundation for ethical thought will never be absolute, but will always be relative to a specific cultural tradition (of the elitism, for example, that Irwin finds so disturbing in Aristotle) and can only be judged adequately within that tradition. As Broadie puts it, "[O]nce the conditions for reflection take hold, the good status quo cannot in fact survive in its original form, but is preserved only by becoming the basis of a life-style centered on an altogether different kind of good."[43]

Both Irwin and Broadie, moreover, characterize the structure of this critical dialectic in primarily formal terms, just as I have suggested that the concept of the appropriate serves a formal, rather than a substantive, limit on action.[44] Broadie, for instance, describes "practical intelligence" *(nous)* as "the disposition, namely, of desiring the formal *best*, which in any given case receives a specified content, but different content from case to case."[45] Somewhat later she says of the moral syllogism based on such moral intuitions that "the agent can have no reason why the argument which completes itself to his satisfaction is a satisfactory argument—which is the same as to say that he can have no reason why the factors which figure as his reasons for the action chosen *are* reasons for it. For another agent they might not be, but the difference is due to a difference in moral perspective."[46] Now, this cannot mean that the moral syllogism is not formally the same, but only that the particular premises, the reasons, will not themselves have any absolute grounding beyond the particular moral perspective, that is, the traditional values and common beliefs, of the individual or group engaged in moral reasoning.

This claim of a formalism in Aristotle's ethics, with regard to the problem of determining the final good, Irwin connects with what he takes to be a similar formalism in Kant. "We may compare Kant's attempt to argue from general features of moral agency and from the necessary features of any moral principle, to definite conclusions about

---

43. Broadie, *Ethics with Aristotle*, 24. On this "hermeneutical" aspect of Aristotle's ethics, see also Gadamer, *Truth and Method*, 312–24.
44. Gadamer suggests that Aristotle's virtues also function only as "schemata" that can be "concretized only in the concrete situation of the person acting" (*Truth and Method*, 320).
45. Broadie, *Ethics with Aristotle*, 252.
46. Broadie, *Ethics with Aristotle*, 253

the character of the only morally acceptable moral principle. We might say that in a similar way Aristotle tries to argue from the form of rational agency to the character of the virtuous moral agent."[47] So long as the *eidos,* or form, of rational agency remains only one possible metaphysical claim about human life, this approach will generate different substantive results, for example, Aristotle's and Kant's views about the role of pleasure in the final human good, but it will remain a strictly formal approach to the evaluation of large-scale claims about the appropriateness of classes of actions, that is, of the virtues one might recommend. Both here and in Broadie, such a formalistic reading of Aristotle seems to have two sources that parallel my own argument for a formal understanding of the use of the concept of the appropriate: first, the lack of a foundation on which to ground clear and substantive rules limiting the kinds of judgments that might be made and, second, a reluctance to accept as given at least some of the actual substantive judgments that Aristotle makes. With no necessary tie between those ethical conclusions and his metaphysics, we are not compelled to accept such judgments, even if we accept the desirability of his formal system for rationalizing our beliefs about appropriate action.

A reading somewhat similar to this can be found in Martha Nussbaum's discussion of Aristotle in *The Fragility of Goodness.* There she argues for what she calls Aristotle's ethical "anthropomorphism," which she is eager to distinguish from any simple relativism,[48] despite the fact that she goes on to note that the *phainomena* in his account are based primarily on his own and closely related cultural traditions because they have a common moral vocabulary that makes such investigation possible.[49] For Aristotle, according to Nussbaum, philosophy requires a critical study based on the double, if not contradictory, standards of consistency and congruence with existing moral belief, but she also admits that in ethics "our beliefs about practice do *not* yield the demand for a deductive system."[50] In a fascinating note, Nussbaum offers a scenario for contested moral decision making on the Aristotelian model that would also provide a paradigm for determining appro-

---

47. Irwin, *Aristotle's First Principles,* 360–61.
48. Martha Nussbaum, *The Fragility of Goodness: Luck and Ethics in Greek Tragedy and Philosophy* (New York: Cambridge University Press, 1986), 242 n. †.
49. Nussbaum, *The Fragility of Goodness,* 245–46.
50. Nussbaum, *The Fragility of Goodness,* 250, emphasis in the original.

priate behavior: one must find some common end that all parties to the dispute would agree on, which would necessarily be a "thinner and more general characterization" of that end than any of those held by the specific parties, and then evaluate the claims of the parties on the basis of how well they satisfy that end.[51] Thus the Madwoman could be said to condemn the "types" of modernity on the basis of a thinner, that is, more abstract conception of justice—one based in turn on the conditions necessary for the flourishing of human life—than that provided by the legal system, which is in the grasp of the "types" themselves, or by the pure revenge suggested by some of the vagabonds.

There are thus three different strands of argument one can trace here with regard to Aristotle. One centers on the concern shared by Irwin, Broadie, and Nussbaum to offer coherent and correct readings of Aristotle's text that would counter many of the contemporary criticisms and misinterpretations of his work. Another centers on whether Aristotle is in fact correct in what he says, which seems not to be the case with his metaphysics, but is arguably the case in his ethics, at least according to these three commentators. Neither of these is something on which I am really qualified to comment, although I am clearly sympathetic to both. My own argument is more minimal; it is that, in any case, the relationship between Aristotle's ethics and his metaphysics seems not to be one of foundation and logical entailment. The *Nicomachean Ethics* would seem to offer us, instead, a nonfoundational concept of appropriate action.

The Appropriate Duty

Heidegger accuses Kant of making an error of exactly the sort that Aristotle (inadvertently) fails to make. In his attempt to ground his ethics on his metaphysics, Heidegger believes that Kant collapses, not Being into beings, but human existence into nonhuman being: "[T]he person is also viewed by Kant as at bottom an extant entity."[52] This is because "we have no self-*intuition* of our self, but all intuition, all immediate giving of something, moves within the forms of space and

---

51. Nussbaum, *The Fragility of Goodness*, 479–80 n. 22.
52. Heidegger, *Basic Problems of Phenomenology*, 148.

time."[53] Kant wants to define the noumenal self as both free and an end-in-itself, but Heidegger would say that such determinations have no basis, given that for Kant the noumenal self lies outside the experienced world of time and space. While "Kant sees clearly the impossibility of conceiving the ego as something extant,"[54] he has no other way to make the moral self determinate, and so remains trapped in traditional ontology. At times Kant seems to agree with such a reading of the relationship between his metaphysics and his ethics, warning that in its search for a foundation for the moral law, "reason should not flap its wings impotently, without leaving the spot, in a space that for it is empty, namely, the space of transcendent concepts that is called the intelligible world, and thereby lose itself among mere phantoms of the brain" (462).[55] If the noumenal is inaccessible to reason, Kant's acknowledgment that there is in his ethics "a sort of circle from which, so it seems, there is no way to escape" (450) seems to survive, rather than submit to, the logic of his metaphysics.

1

In response to Hume's skeptical empiricism, Kant's metaphysics divides reality into two spheres: one experienced, or phenomenal; the other intelligible, or noumenal. This allows him to relegate Hume's arguments to the experienced realm and to answer skepticism with reference to the intelligible. It is important to note, however, that this is a new kind of dualism, as distinct from both modern and Platonic mind/body dualisms as it is from the immanent dualism of form and matter in Aristotle. Nor is it another version of the difference between the apparent and the real. The phenomenal world *is* real in the sense that there is nothing more real from which it is derived. What it is derived from is something more primary, but in itself largely unknowable. The noumenal and phenomenal are not distinct realities, but different ways of understanding the same reality. Thus, for Kant there can be a valid phenomenal science of the mind (psychology) as well as a noumenal aspect to material reality, the things-in-themselves.

53. Heidegger, *Basic Problems of Phenomenology*, 145, emphasis in the original.
54. Heidegger, *Basic Problems of Phenomenology*, 147.
55. Immanuel Kant, *Grounding for the Metaphysics of Morals*, trans. James W. Ellington (Indianapolis: Hackett, 1981), 61. Hereafter references to this text will be made by marginal page numbers in parentheses.

Moreover, the relationship between these two aspects of human existence is far more subtle and complex than the simple dominance of mind over body, knowledge over appearance, that one finds in Plato or Descartes. It is, in fact, this relationship that provides the key both to Kant's ethics and to his epistemological response to Hume. Kant is able to avoid Hume's skeptical conclusions by showing in great detail how the intelligibility of the noumenal realm explains the laws that govern our experience of the world. As he says, *"[T]he understanding does not derive its laws (a priori) from, but prescribes them to, nature."*[56]

The means of this derivation is through a category of logical relation that Kant believes he has discovered in mathematics and geometry, the possibility of synthetic a priori knowledge. For him, mathematics is neither a matter of pure logic (as Hume believed) nor very high-level abstract empirical generalization (as Mill believed). Instead, mathematical and geometrical relationships are necessary truths, not about the world as it might be in itself, but about any possible human experience of the world, any possible phenomena. The failure of empiricist accounts of mathematics (as well as the rationalist account relying on innate ideas) provides a clue to the failure of empiricism to avoid Hume's skepticism. Not only must all phenomena follow the laws of time and space that underlie math and geometry, Kant goes on to argue, any experience that can be accommodated into an objective human reality must also follow other laws that correspond to other limitations on human rational process, most notably the laws of cause and effect and substantial relations. What neither a priori analytic knowledge nor a posteriori synthetic knowledge can explain is those laws that mediate between the two in the form of a priori synthetic knowledge. The failure of philosophers up to his time to recognize this, Kant suggests, is due to the fact that these laws have their existence in the noumenal realm, and so are accessible only after a thorough critique of the normal use of human reason, a critique necessitated by Hume and carried out by Kant himself.

This, then, is the metaphysical underpinning of Kant's moral philosophy. The basic claim of his ethics is that the moral law, in the form of the categorical imperative, is, like the law of cause and effect, an a

---

56. Immanuel Kant, *Prolegomena for Any Future Metaphysics,* trans. James W. Ellington (Indianapolis: Hackett, 1977), 62, italics in the original.

priori synthetic law of pure reason that governs, not our phenomenal understanding of the world, but how we ought to act in that world. The primary difference between the two cases, however, lies in the fact that the phenomena of human experience, and the failure of either empiricism or rationalism satisfactorily to account for those phenomena, provide a strong foundation for accepting the possibility of a priori synthetic knowledge. Our only choice, as Kant is fond of pointing out, is between his metaphysics and the chaos of Humean skepticism.[57] In the moral sphere, however, things are not quite so clear. The only phenomena that could validate, if not prove, the existence of an a priori synthetic law of absolute duty would be acts exemplifying such a duty, but such exemplars are ruled out as impossible by the very hiddenness of motives in the noumenal realm: "In fact there is absolutely no possibility by means of experience to make out with complete certainty a single case in which the maxim of an action that may in other respects conform to duty has rested solely on moral grounds and on the representation of one's duty" (*Grounding for the Metaphysics of Morals*, 406). Thus the empirical grounds that provide at least some basis of plausibility, albeit a negative one, for the epistemological consequences of Kant's thought are entirely lacking in his ethics.

What Kant offers to substitute for empirical, scientific grounds in the ethical realm are two aspects of human experience that seem closer to "feelings," our sense of moral obligation and our sense of our own freedom, which seem to function as the underlying conditions for the categorical imperative much as time and space function as the underlying conditions for the categories. In the *Grounding of the Metaphysics of Morals* he offers "the Ordinary Knowledge of Morality" as the basis for the transition, first, to "Popular Moral Philosophy," then to "a Metaphysics of Morals," and finally to "a Critique of Practical Reason" (392), relying, much like Aristotle, on his audience's existing moral sense to ground his ethical system. Also like Aristotle, it is human rationality that Kant uses as the basis for his transition from one to the other. The concept of a duty that is rational in nature and transcends all human inclination already "dwells in the natural sound understanding and needs not so much to be taught as merely to be elucidated" (397). This leads, in the "Metaphysics of Morals," to the dictate that "rational nature exists as an end in itself. In this way man necessarily thinks of

---

57. For instance, see Kant, *Prolegomena*, 91.

his own existence" (429) and from there to the form of the categorical imperative called the formula of the end-in-itself.

Note that to make his point Kant relies here on the empirical fact that we do see ourselves in certain ways. This suggests two possible problems with his view. First, the empirical universality of a sense of moral obligation as the underlying form of our ethical life might be less self-evident than the universality of time and space in sensory experience. Second, again as in Aristotle, Kant opens himself to empirical challenge about the specific content of such moral experience, even if the form were proved to be universal. What if our sense of ourselves as rational in this way were merely an artifact of our cultural understanding of the human, such that other traditions might, for instance, see the end of human existence as some divine plan, not our own rationality, and regard our lives as determined in advance by that same plan? Moral intuitions seem not to be enough to decide between such alternative understandings of human moral experience.

The argument for freedom of the will relies on the fact that we can act only as if we are free. "Now I say that every being which cannot act in any way other than under the idea of freedom is for this very reason free from a practical point of view" (448). Our actions assume freedom, so, for all practical purposes, we are free because denying our freedom would make no difference in our experience, just as for Hume causal necessity functions in everyday life despite the lack of any adequate rational justification for our belief in it.[58] Such an argument for freedom would seem to be another empirical claim about human experience, subject to the doubts raised by posthypnotic suggestion, addiction, or obsessive/compulsive disorders. Kant argues that freedom can be derived from human rationality: if we were not free in this way, our rationality, and thus the ability to know our moral duty, would serve no purpose, since our actions would be caused by something else. At the same time, however, he says that our actions can always *also* be explained entirely in terms of empirical causal laws (451–52). The sphere of free will seems sharply limited to the noumenal, and so is subject to at least two objections: (1) there is no noumenal realm; (2) if we accept such a realm on epistemological grounds, we might still not be free, because, to take Spinoza's version, our noumenal existence could be a manifestation of God that has no independent will of its

---

58. Hume, *Enquiry Concerning Human Understanding*, 110–11.

own. Neither our "ordinary" sense of moral duty nor the fact that we must act as if we were free seems to provide a basis for Kant's ethical thought comparable to the basis that everyday experience of an orderly natural world provides for his epistemological thought.

2

Thus, although neither Kant's epistemology nor his ethics can be, strictly speaking, proved independently of his account of the noumenal/phenomenal split, the proof of which in turn rests to some extent on its ability to solve basic epistemological and ethical problems, the plausibility of his claims about our knowledge of the world is of a significantly different quality from the plausibility of his claims about free will and moral duty. Kant himself is, of course, very aware of this difference. While he never explicitly suggests that his epistemological claims rely on a certain level of circularity, he clearly acknowledges that his ethical arguments fall short of an absolute proof. He notes in the preface to the *Critique of Practical Reason,* for instance, that "had not the moral law already been distinctly thought in our reasons, we would never have been justified in assuming anything like freedom, even though it is not self-contradictory. But if there were no freedom, the moral law would never have been encountered in us."[59] If one denies the existence of a moral law of the kind Kant describes, a moral skepticism that may seem more plausible than Hume's epistemological skepticism, there seems no way into, or out of, this circle. The noumenal realm is radically unknowable, except by the way in which it conditions our experience of the phenomenal world. This means of access seems to be lacking in the case of practical reason, where the "thought of an intelligible world is merely negative as regards the world of sense" (*Grounding for the Metaphysics of Morals,* 458). The "sort of circle" in Kant's logic here seems to be irreducible, a case of "pure dialectic" in Irwin's terms, where common beliefs are refined, but without providing any deeper metaphysical base.

Many of Kant's commentators seem to feel no need, or are unable, to re-create his thought in such a way as to fill in this gap in its logic. In *Imagination and Interpretation in Kant,* for example, one use Rudolf

---

59. Immanuel Kant, *Critique of Practical Reason,* trans. Lewis White Beck (New York: Macmillan, 1956), 4n.

Makkreel wants to make of Kant's aesthetics is to provide a supplemental account of the unity of the moral subject in Kant because, as suggested by the Heidegger quotations above, "the satisfactory treatment of the subject as a whole remains an unfulfilled task in his philosophy."[60] Paul Crowther's book on Kant's aesthetics also cites this problem: "Now this area of Kant's philosophy is, unfortunately, deeply problematic, inasmuch as the relations between the phenomenal self, the formal unity of consciousness, and the supersensible [noumenal] self are never adequately clarified by him. Indeed, in terms of consistency with his overall Critical epistemology Kant can only give the supersensible self a negative characterization."[61] In *The Differend,* Jean-François Lyotard explicitly traces Kant's circular reasoning from freedom to the possibility of a moral law: "What can be deducted in the absence of the law is freedom. This new deduction is carried out starting from the law. But the law is then placed, within the justificatory argument, not as a conclusion, ... but rather as a premise." For Lyotard, therefore, it is clear that "this Idea can be neither proven nor refuted, even though there are the greatest practical reasons to admit the principle of freedom."[62]

Henry Allison, by contrast, argues in *Kant's Theory of Freedom* that the admitted "circle" in the *Grounding of the Metaphysics of Morals* was importantly rethought in the *Critique of Practical Reason*. His claim is that although the argument in the second *Critique* "will hardly persuade the critic who rejects the basic thrust of Kant's moral theory, ... it does suffice to remove the specter of moral skepticism for someone who accepts the analysis of morality offered in the first two parts of the *Groundwork*."[63] He accomplishes even this rather limited defense of Kant, however, only by insisting on a nonmetaphysical understanding of what I have taken as Kant's basic metaphysical innovation, the noumenal/phenomenal split. Allison calls this position a "two-aspect" view of this split, as contrasted with "the familiar 'two-object' or 'two-world' interpretation."[64] He says, for instance, that despite ref-

60. Rudolf Makkreel, *Imagination and Interpretation in Kant* (Chicago: University of Chicago Press, 1990), 84.
61. Paul Crowther, *The Kantian Sublime: From Morality to Art* (New York: Oxford University Press, 1989), 17.
62. Jean-François Lyotard, *The Differend: Phrases in Dispute,* trans. Georges Van Den Abbeele (Minneapolis: University of Minnesota Press, 1988), 120 and 134.
63. Henry E. Allison, *Kant's Theory of Freedom* (New York: Cambridge University Press, 1990), 3.
64. Allison, *Kant's Theory of Freedom,* 4.

erences to "a subject's 'intelligible existence'" in the second *Critique,* Kant "is not propounding a noumenalistic metaphysics but simply describing how subjects, qua responsible moral agents, must take themselves."[65] That is, rational human agents not only experience themselves phenomenally, as subject to interests, needs, and desires, but also see themselves from a standpoint where they can, indeed must, choose which of those interests, needs, and desires will become operative in the (phenomenal) choices that they make. For Allison, the rules according to which we make such choices are maxims, "self-imposed, practical principle[s] or rule[s] of action."[66]

As rational agents, moreover, we must taken the maxims we adopt as in some sense justified, which Allison considers key to the derivation of the categorical imperative in the third part of the *Grounding of the Metaphysics of Morals* because, "in claiming that one's reason for acting in a certain way is a 'good' in the sense of justifying reason, one is, implicitly at least, assuming its appropriateness for all rational beings."[67] Thus his interpretation seems to suggest an account of moral deliberation that would assimilate Kant's ethical thought to Aristotle's concept of *sophrosune* and hence, indirectly at least, to the concept of the appropriate as defined here. In her "constructivist" reading of Kant in *Constructions of Reason,* Onora O'Neill likewise suggests a mode of moral reasoning in Kant that would bring it closer to the concept of the appropriate than to the usual "algorithmic" account of Kant. She traces the political metaphors in Kant's thought to argue that in both the cognitive and political orders "we have a plurality of agents or voices . . . and no transcendent or preestablished authority. Authority has in either case to be constructed."[68] That construction can, however, be neither transcendentally grounded nor strictly logical, because "any thinking or decision making that actually follows algorithms . . . depends on some specific and perhaps groundless premises that permit a decisive selection of well-formed formulae and valid inferences."[69] Again, the model is one of a formal or "pure" dialectic within a specific context, rather than deduction from transcendent truths.

65. Allison, *Kant's Theory of Freedom,* 141.
66. Allison, *Kant's Theory of Freedom,* 89.
67. Allison, *Kant's Theory of Freedom,* 204.
68. Onora O'Neill, *Constructions of Reason: Explorations of Kant's Practical Philosophy* (New York: Cambridge University Press, 1989), 16.
69. O'Neill, *Constructions of Reason,* 19. (Cf. Broadie on the *orthos logos* in Aristotle, page 40 above.)

O'Neill also bases her reading of Kant on a "two-aspect" view of the noumenal/phenomenal split. She finds the key move in the third section of the *Grounding* to be the shift, not to "an unconditional transcendent vantage point," but to "a critical view of the starting point, or condition, of one's own previous thinking," a shift parallel to that Kant makes in reconciling the antinomies of pure reason in the *Prolegomena to Any Future Metaphysics*.[70] For her, Kant is seeking, not absolute first principles, but "principles that do not fail even if used universally and reflexively."[71] Further, she suggests that the "two standpoints" humans must take are a sign of *"the finitude, not the transcendence, of human reason"* because, "[a]lthough the empirical use of reason must strive for completeness in naturalistic understanding, the completeness is only a regulative ideal, and not attainable."[72] For Allison, a parallel distinction between a duty to strive and a duty to attain in Kant's *Doctrine of Virtue* means that the impossibility of achieving holiness eliminates the need for its metaphysical conditions, "the postulate of immortality, God's intellectual intuition, and grace."[73] If we can, and must, do no more than strive for complete understanding or a good will, that is, if we can only strive for a life of intellectual virtue guided by *sophrosune* in the Aristotelian sense, then Kant's ethics can be saved, but, as with Aristotle, only at the expense of a strong (i.e., "two-worlds") reading of his metaphysics. Even Allison must admit morality and freedom might both be illusory, although he insists they cannot be taken as such "from a practical point of view."[74]

None of this, therefore, would weaken the claim that ultimately Kantian ethics is nonfoundational, that is, is either not entailed by his metaphysics alone, if the noumenal/phenomenal split is taken in a strong sense, because of the inaccessibility of the noumenal, or can be reduced to something much like *sophrosune*, if the noumenal and phenomenal are taken in a nonmetaphysical sense as "two aspects" of a common reality. This parallel between Aristotle's ethics and his own would undoubtedly be an unwelcome insight for Kant—even if he might acknowledge the tenuous logical relationship between his ethics and his metaphysics—because of his deep distrust of any morality

70. Kant, *Prolegomena*, 82–84.
71. O'Neill, *Constructions of Reason*, 56.
72. O'Neill, *Constructions of Reason*, 61, italics in the original.
73. Allison, *Kant's Theory of Freedom*, 175.
74. Allison, *Kant's Theory of Freedom*, 247.

based on "happiness." He would agree with the earlier argument, and Aristotle's concession, that such a morality cannot provide the kind of moral rules that Kant seeks. "The principle of happiness can indeed give maxims, but never maxims which are competent to be laws of the will, even if universal happiness were made the object. For, since the knowledge of this rests on mere data of experience, as each judgment concerning it depends very much on the very changeable opinion of each person, it can give general but never universal rules."[75] At the same time, it is not clear that Kant can give the necessary rules, at least not substantive ones. The categorical imperative, like the categories, seems to provide nothing more than a formal schema of duty, or appropriate action, without clear concrete content until specific contextualized empirical grounds, including cultural values, are given for choice.

Kwasi Wiredu, for instance, offers a theory of moral universals based on what he calls "the principle of sympathetic impartiality"—"Let your conduct at all times manifest a due concern for the interests of others"—which he notes bears a strong resemblance to the categorical imperative with "a dose of compassion."[76] He adopts this principle in part on the un-Kantian ground that "it is essential to the harmonization of human interests in society," but also considers it well founded on both the theory and practice of traditional Akan society.[77] He later characterizes Akan culture as "humanistic" because it is based on human interests, as contrasted with both the ethical supernaturalism of traditional Christianity and the nonhumanism he finds in Kantian deontology.[78] He offers these very different metaphysical and cultural commitments as the basis for a moral universal that remains highly Kantian, in form at least. In content, however, it may be a different story. One specific universal Wiredu cites is "chastity,"[79] a moral concept he would want to distinguish from the various customs that would define the exact meaning of the term. Thus, his account of traditional Akan attitudes toward premarital sexual relations (while not unlike the eighteenth-and nineteenth-century practice in the rural American

75. Kant, *Critique of Practical Reason*, 37.
76. Kwasi Wiredu, *Cultural Universals and Particulars: An African Perspective* (Bloomington: Indiana University Press, 1996), 29.
77. Wiredu, *Cultural Universals and Particulars*, 29.
78. Wiredu, *Cultural Universals and Particulars*, 65.
79. Wiredu, *Cultural Universals and Particulars*, 30.

South, where circuit-riding preachers often performed weddings and the baptism of firstborns on the same visit) would undoubtedly have violated Kant's Pietist sense of chastity, to put it mildly.[80] Thus, different metaphysics can generate the same formal ethical principle, but result in very different concrete practices in different cultural contexts.

In those cases where Kant does give specific content to the categorical imperative, the "perfect duties," such as the duty to keep one's promises, their concrete content can be attributed to their institutional nature; that is, they rely on a commitment to the maintenance of a particular social institution as a substantive premise for the formal argument.[81] Other perfect duties, such as the prohibition against suicide, are not institutional and may also fail to convince, for example, in the case of a suicide in the face of certain but slow and painful death. In Kant's case of "a man reduced to despair," suicide amounts to a case of making life better by making it impossible, a manifest self-contradiction (*Grounding for the Metaphysics of Morals*, 421–22). In the case I suggested, however, suicide is made at least arguably appropriate because it is a case of ending sooner a life that is doomed in any case—there is no contradiction here and hence no clear rule. His imperfect duties seem even more open to such objections. Does failure to develop one's talents constitute a serious breach of one's moral duties, of some possible "natural law"? What if one chose instead to devote oneself to charity, as did Mother Teresa, or to raising one's children, as women did in Kant's day? Are "South Sea Islanders" (423) necessarily moral sinners? The imperfect duty to benevolence provides an interesting contrast with Aristotle, who considered "liberality" and even "magnificence" to be virtues. Which of these accounts are we to accept? Clearly the answer cannot lie in the categorical imperative, but only in what is appropriate in the cultural contexts these philosophers represent.

On the other hand, what people these days might take as the most important "perfect" duties, or duties without exception (422n), such as the duty not to murder or rape, do not count as perfect duties for Kant

---

80. Wiredu, *Cultural Universals and Particulars*, 72–74.
81. This category would also include, minimally, prohibitions against lying, theft (according to Hume, *An Enquiry Concerning Human Understanding*, 113), and arguably at least some forms of murder. For the broader argument, see the last chapter of John Searle's *Speech Acts* (New York: Cambridge University Press, 1969).

and might perhaps not even be imperfect ones, since they can be argued to entail no contradiction either of logic or of the will (424). Is there any such contradiction in murdering someone else in order to live better, except perhaps insofar as refraining from killing others has become institutionalized as part of a political system? Even in that case, murdering those who are outside of such a system, slaves or "the enemy," could still be permissible, or even mandatory. While he might wish to preclude such actions as treating "humanity" in those killed only as means to one's ends, his reliance on rationality as the criterion of "humanity" means that the scope of the prohibition would depend on who was considered rational, that is, on what was appropriate within a particular tradition. Similarly, rape can be, and has been, considered as a kind of theft, in which case it becomes an institutional duty not to rape, but again one that does not apply outside the confines of property law, that is, to slaves, prostitutes, or the enemy's women. An appeal to treating others as ends in themselves would rule rape out, again, only if women were recognized as rational. Some of Kant's moral intuitions, like Aristotle's, are now out of date or out of fashion, which does not invalidate the categorical imperative as a formal criterion of appropriate action, but does show it to be purely formal, in need of specific institutions or practices to give it content.

This formalism in Kant's ethics is a central point in Robin Schott's feminist critique of his work. She relates it to the individualist, asocial world in which all of Kant's philosophy operates, which she sees in turn as a manifestation of the modern capitalist world, a rejection of women's role in that world and of the body: "In his view, moral principles are universally valid, independent of the content of any particular social situation. But the very formality of the Kantian moral law reflects the reification experienced by individuals in bourgeois society."[82] While agreeing with Schott's critique, I am, however, as uncomfortable with reading Marx back into Kant as with reading Aristotle's dualism as if it were Plato's. In the modern world the move to the formal does have gender implications, and class implications as well. Sometimes, however, it is necessary, for instance, if there is no content that one could give to a moral principle that would not immediately announce its status as a justification of the conventions of one's society, as, at

---

82. Robin May Schott, *Cognition and Eros: A Critique of the Kantian Paradigm* (Boston: Beacon Press, 1988), 138.

best, a rationalized concept of appropriate action. Even Aristotle, who could not have been a capitalist, even if he was a sexist, had no alternative. The only possible alternative, as I have argued, is to develop a metaphysics to provide a determinate end for human life and derive the content of one's moral beliefs from that. What I would suggest is that, for all its benign results for feminism, such a foundational approach, in utilitarianism and arguably in Plato as well, in and of itself is no more a friend to feminism than Kant's impersonal, capitalist, and thoroughly masculine concept of appropriate action.

In Kant, as in Aristotle, the supposed metaphysical foundation is insufficient to provide a logical grounding for the ethics. Kant's distinction between the noumenal and phenomenal realms subverts ethics, instead of supporting it, by rendering impossible both the knowledge that would tie it to metaphysics and any phenomenal manifestations of moral action that could lend it credence. Noumenally, human existence could be free and, by Kant's standards, irrational (as it is, perhaps, in Mill), rational and unfree (as in Spinoza), or unfree and irrational (as for Hume). If it is rational and reason serves a purpose, it must be free—and vice versa. "But how freedom is possible, and how we should think theoretically and positively of this type of causality is not thereby discovered."[83] The noumenal self might generate a very different ethical system if it were understood as a creature of a Creator whose rationality existed only to further the divine plan or as a social self whose primary duties were understood collectively rather than individualistically (as in the *Republic*). This failure to ground his ethical thought in his metaphysics is revealed in Kant's parallel failure to provide substantive rules for moral action. The categorical imperative remains a formal principle, a way to rationalize a sense of appropriate action subject to variation based on the concrete circumstances of the case and, more problematically for Kant, on the social context in which it appears. There are few examples in Kant, and no foundations. To make a moral rule for oneself based on the fact that its maxim could become a law for all rational beings in exactly the same situation is to make no rule at all; it is only to rationalize what one already knows to be one's duty.

Earlier I claimed that the Madwoman's reason for condemning the President and his minions was not grounded in any Kantian Universal

---

83. Kant, *Critique of Practical Reason*, 138.

or Aristotelian virtue, any more than it was grounded in some utilitarian benefit or Platonic Goodness. In this chapter I have not backed away from that position, but rather have tried to gain credence for the Madwoman's own reasons from the fact that, while quite different in form, they are not different in kind from the reasons that Kant or Aristotle might be able to give in a similar situation. Understanding rationality as the essence of human existence is not entailed by understanding humans to have a formal essence, nor does it necessarily entail a unique solution to the Madwoman's problem. Understanding human existence as primarily noumenal by definition tells us nothing about the nature of that existence, nor does the categorical imperative dictate that the Madwoman and her friends either tolerate or destroy those who seek to destroy them. If the Madwoman's reasons seem to have no absolute metaphysical basis, she is in good philosophical company.

Interlude

What Is Appropriate Now?

At this point, it seems necessary also to suggest in greater detail how the concept of the appropriate might actually function in a given moral situation. Of course, I have already offered two examples of the use of the concept of the appropriate in ethical thought. On the one hand, the very abstract and indeed fanciful story of the Madwoman of Chaillot has been offered as a case of due and proper consideration of what is the appropriate course of action in her obviously fictitious situation. On the other hand, I have suggested that the all too real practice of ritual female genital mutilation provides a sort of opposite pole or test case in which the proper functioning of the concept of the appropriate must entail a definite result, although I consider myself completely unqualified, for a whole host of reasons, to make the hermeneutical and pragmatic studies that would prove my own point.

As my example here, therefore, I have chosen a somewhat more accessible case of what might be considered an inappropriate practice, one that can serve as a mean between these other two more extreme cases.[1] The principled refusal of the Roman Catholic Church to ordain woman is a real-life situation that causes real women real pain, but it is a pain of a kind that I, along with many women my age and older, might find familiar from our own experiences of exclusion based on gender. It is also an institutional issue that arises from a cultural tradition in which I might be considered a reasonably well-informed outsider, based both on my professional training in the texts on which the Catholic Church rests much of its doctrine, and on my religious training in the Episcopal Church, which still considers itself to be within the "catholic and apostolic" tradition but which has also recently begun to ordain women.[2]

In this interlude, therefore, I investigate, first, the deep textual sources on which the decision not to ordain women seems primarily to be based, in a still preliminary and partial study of this practice, and, second, the failure of other concepts of what is appropriate—those based on Enlightenment liberalism, for instance—truly to engage the Catholic Church's position in such a way as to generate genuine dialogue and, with it, the possibility of eventual change. In so doing, I hope to maintain the proper hermeneutical stance described by Hans-Georg Gadamer: "I must allow tradition's claim to validity, not in the sense of simply acknowledging the past in its otherness, but in such a way that it has something to say to me. This too calls for a fundamental sort of openness."[3]

1

A call to the local seminary reveals an interesting list of qualifications for the Roman Catholic priesthood: a master's degree in divinity or theology (which also serves in this situation as a de facto intelligence

---

1. Again, "inappropriate" might be considered too weak a word here, but as noted earlier, I intend to use it in a quasi-technical sense as a term in "ethical theory," as defined in the Conclusion.
2. In writing this section, however, I have also relied on the helpful comments of Timothy Polk, my colleague in religion at Hamline, Gale Yee of the Theology Department of the University of Saint Thomas (St. Paul, Minnesota), and Glenn S. Holland, holder of the Bishop James Mills Thoburn Chair of Religious Studies at Allegheny College, none of whom holds any responsibility for the final form of my argument.
3. Hans-Georg Gadamer, *Truth and Method,* 2d ed., trans. Joel Weinsheimer and Donald G. Marshall (New York: Crossroad Press, 1989), 361.

requirement) plus membership in the church and active participation in parish life for at least two years. The informant points out that these requirements may be different for other dioceses, for the various religious orders, and so on, and adds that ordination in this diocese also calls for an intensive parish "internship" and extensive psychological and behavioral testing. She does not add, although the questioner is clearly female, that candidates for ordination must be men. Presumably any intelligent woman already knows that.

The *New Catholic Encyclopedia* lists similar requirements, but points out that candidates for the priesthood must be "legitimate or legitimated men" with a solid hope of permanent service to the Catholic Church. Ruled out would be "[t]roublemakers, the rebellious and incorrigible, and those whose character, morals, or intellectual deficiencies render them unfit for the priesthood."[4] If these are the qualities that make men ineligible, it is not difficult to see why some women view their exclusion from the priesthood as a sign of subordinate status within the church, based on some sort of inherent deficiency or defect.

Richard P. McBrien's book *Catholicism* lists five arguments against the ordination of women. Of these, three rely on the traditions of the Catholic Church as their primary basis, and one rebuts the claim that women have a right to ordination by pointing out that no one has such a right.[5] Appeals to the tradition, however, have a certain air of circularity in a discussion based on the premise that the tradition may have been in error, and also beg the question of alternative interpretations of the tradition (a point to which I will return). Therefore, I will focus my application of the concept of the appropriate on McBrien's remaining argument: "The ordained priest must act in the name of Christ, and, therefore, must be able to represent him physically as well as spiritually. The Orthodox refer to this as 'iconic' representation."[6]

The arguments offered in the Vatican's 1976 "Declaration on the Question of the Admission of Women to the Ministerial Priesthood" follow a similar pattern, with a few variations. Again, the main point that does not rely either on the tradition or on historical or textual interpretation is that the "Christian priesthood is . . . of a sacramental nature: the priest is a sign, the supernatural effectiveness of which

---

4. *New Catholic Encyclopedia* (New York: McGraw-Hill, 1967), 13:71.
5. Richard P. McBrien, *Catholicism* (Minneapolis, Minn.: Winston Press, 1981), 853.
6. McBrien, *Catholicism*, 853.

comes from the ordination received, but a sign that must be perceptible and which the faithful must be able to recognize with ease."[7] The argument would be that, just as the wine in the Mass cannot simply be replaced with grape juice (as is done in some American Protestant churches), because the physical attributes of the elements are themselves part of their effectiveness as sign, so the (male) physical presence of Jesus cannot be replaced in the Mass with a female body. The question then is how women are like grape juice or, what is more relevant, how this focus on the masculine physicality of Jesus and of priests is related to the stated exclusion from ordination of those whose "character, morals, or intellectual deficiencies" would render them unfit for the priesthood. To answer that question requires a long excursus through a wide variety of texts.

All of Christianity shares a basic dilemma with regard to women, one that is clearly laid out in a rather quaint collection of quotations from Saint Thomas Aquinas selected by H. C. O'Neill at the turn of the century. In it, O'Neill quotes Aquinas as saying, in the same place, that "[b]oth in man and woman is to be found the image of God, as to that in which the essence of the image principally consists, that is, as to the intellectual nature," with a reference to Gen. 1:27, but also that "in a secondary sense the image of God is in man in a sense in which it does not exist in woman," for "man is the beginning and end of woman, as God is the beginning and end of every creature," here with reference to 1 Cor. 11:7–9.[8] What this quotation illustrates is that from its earliest origins Christianity has carried a double legacy of gender equity and male domination.[9] Nor can this legacy be neatly divided into spiritual equality and temporal patriarchy, since the above quotation explicitly ties both sides of this paradox to the "intellectual nature" of both men and women.[10]

---

7. "Declaration on the Question of the Admission of Women to the Ministerial Priesthood," in *Women Priests: A Catholic Commentary on the Vatican Declaration,* ed. Leonard Swidler and Arlene Swidler (New York: Paulist Press, 1977), 43.

8. H. C. O'Neill, *New Things and Old in Saint Thomas Aquinas* (London: Dent & Co., 1909), 302.

9. I mean "earliest" here both textually (the quite different versions of the creation of man and woman in Genesis 1 and 2) and historically (the quite different views on women in the Christian Bible that can be attributed to Jesus and Saint Paul, on the one hand, and to Paul's later pseudonymous imitators, on the other).

10. For an account of how these views were played out in the earlier history of the church, see Rosemary Radford Ruether's "Misogynism and Virginal Feminism in the Fathers of the Church," in *Religion and Sexism,* ed. Rosemary Radford Ruether (New York: Simon & Schuster, 1974), 150–83.

The importance of the physical "iconic representation" of the male priest can perhaps be traced from the difference between Aquinas's formulation above and the text he cites from Saint Paul: "For the man is not of woman but the woman of man; and the man was not created for woman, but the woman for man" (1 Cor. 11:8–9). Whereas Paul's explanation is, from a philosophical perspective at least, rather vague, the quotation from Aquinas can be given a rather definite philosophical content by reference to Aristotle.

God is "the beginning and end of every creature" as its creator/source and as that for the sake of which it lives. How can the same be true of the relationship between men and women? In Aristotle's account of gender difference, the male element (sperm) carries the form of the fetus, while the female element (menstrual blood) provides its matter. That is, the male is the sole "genetic" parent of the child, while the female provides only the womb as a site of incubation. Thus, men are the "beginning," or creator/source, of all children, male and female. Sexual difference arises only because women (although not necessarily females of other species) are "cooler" than males due to their longer gestation period (ten versus nine months) and resultant lower metabolism. Therefore, "the female state" is "as it were a deformity, though one which occurs in the ordinary course of nature."[11] Aquinas agrees with the Philosopher, at least in the case of the particular, embodied woman: "As regards the individual nature, woman is defective and misbegotten, for the active power in the male seed tends to the production of a perfect likeness according to the masculine sex; while the production of woman comes from defect in the active power, or from some material indisposition, or even from some external influence."[12]

Unhindered by the systematic ambivalence of the Christian tradition, Aristotle's question in the *Metaphysics* (10.9) is based on a strongly perceived inequality between men and woman. He raises the question "why woman does not differ from man in species, since male and female are contrary."[13] His answer there is that they are the same in form, but differ in matter, or body, in the way described above. This

---

11. Aristotle, "On the Generation of Animals," cited in *Philosophy of Woman*, ed. Mary Briody Mahowald (Indianapolis: Hackett, 1983), 271.
12. Saint Thomas Aquinas, *Summa Theologica*, Question 92, First Article, Reply to Objection 1, cited in *Philosophy of Woman*, ed. Mahowald, 277.
13. Aristotle, *Metaphysics*, trans. Richard Hope (Ann Arbor: University of Michigan Press, 1960), 217.

allows Aquinas, if not Aristotle himself, to emphasize the sameness of the "intellectual nature" in men and women that seems inherent in at least some Christian doctrine about gender equality, while maintaining the patriarchal status quo. It also underscores the importance of the material, or bodily, difference between men and women as the locus of the latter's inferiority.

This tells us how man is the beginning of woman, despite strong empirical evidence that the reverse is also true, but not yet why he is also her "end." In this case, the saint and the philosopher are in perfect agreement. In the same article cited above, Aquinas justifies the "civil" subjection of women by saying that "woman is naturally subject to man, because in man the discernment of reason predominates."[14] Similarly, Aristotle states in the *Nicomachean Ethics* (8.10) that marriage is analogous to an aristocracy, "for the man rules in accordance with his [greater] worth."[15] Both there and in the *Politics* he explains that the man's greater capacity for reason means that he is better able to guide the woman, as well as his slaves, to the Good Life, so subjecting them to his control serves their own interests better than allowing them to act freely, guided only by their own (lesser) intellect.[16] Similarly, Aquinas says of the "civil" subordination of women, as opposed to "servile" subjection, that "the superior makes use of his subjects for their own benefit and good."[17] The man is the end of the woman, for he sets her goals in life and enables her to achieve them through his governance, just as God sets His creatures their purposes in life and enables them to achieve those purposed through the laws that He sets down for them.

This, then, is a vision of the world in which men's superior "discernment of reason" is tied, on the one hand, to an underlying similarity in kind (determined by form and *telos*) that mandates their careful guidance of women along the proper path of life and, on the other, to a bodily (material) superiority, or lack of deformity, that, in Aristotle at

---

14. Saint Thomas Aquinas, *Summa Theologica,* Question 92, First Article, Reply to Objection 2, cited in *Philosophy of Woman,* ed. Mahowald, 278.
15. Aristotle, *Nicomachean Ethics,* trans. David Ross (New York: Oxford University Press, 1980), 210.
16. See Aristotle, *The Politics,* trans. T. A. Sinclair (New York: Penguin, 1981), 94–97 (1259b-1260b).
17. Saint Thomas Aquinas, *Summa Theologica,* Question 92, First Article, Reply to Objection 2, cited in *Philosophy of Woman,* ed. Mahowald, 278

least, almost amounts to a difference in kind. On this basis, the bodily differences between the sexes becomes the "icon" of a deep difference in nature such that to serve as the representative of a man, Jesus, one must be a man, albeit one who is not defective with regard to birth (illegitimate), character, morals, or intellect, that is, not defective in those ways *and* also not defective in being a woman. Each individual woman is, as Aquinas says, a "misbegotten" man, and a priest must not be misbegotten, either literally or figuratively. This is the deep message that, I believe, underlies the refusal of the Catholic Church to ordain woman, one that survives from a time when the assertion of the "full Christian and human equality of women with men"[18] was not yet fully recognized, and one that explains, without fully justifying, the centuries-old practices on which the exclusion of women from the priesthood is based.

Many would claim, however, that the 1976 Vatican statement no longer relies on an Aristotelian biology, which now can seem both unbiblical and unscientific, one that "modern thought," the document suggests, might "rightly reject."[19] There are two related ways in which the statement most obviously moves beyond the (necessarily) more simplified arguments in McBrien's summary. The first is in the claim that the sacramental signs (wine, the male body of the priest) are not conventions that might be changed over time but essentially atemporal or ahistorical practices, ways in which "persons of every period" are linked "to the supreme Event of the history of salvation."[20] The declaration also points out the many ways that Jesus and his early followers deviated from the cultural traditions surrounding them in their treatment of women, suggesting that if they had meant that women should be priests, the prejudices of their own time would not have kept them from instituting such a practice. Thus the decision of Jesus and his immediate followers not to ordain women is not due to historically variable factors that might no longer be relevant, but to what the declaration cites Saint Paul as considering, "the divine plan of creation (cf. 1 Cor. 11:7; Gen. 2:18–24)." The declaration then goes on to say that "[i]t would be difficult to see in it the expression of a cultural fact."[21]

18. McBrien, *Catholicism*, 853.
19. "Declaration," in *Women Priests,* ed. Swidler and Swidler, 38.
20. "Declaration," in *Women Priests,* ed. Swidler and Swidler, 42.
21. "Declaration," in *Women Priests,* ed. Swidler and Swidler, 41–42.

The difficulty here is relative to one's interpretation of the more general argument. That is, the independence of this particular practice from historical process seems to depend on what nonhistorical, extracultural basis is provided for it. The case of wine in the Mass is somewhat different because, Prohibition aside, no compelling reason has been presented to challenge the use of this particular sacramental sign. But a case has been made, both by other churches and by elements within Catholicism, that the textual and the historical evidence on which the declaration relies is open to a variety of interpretations, many of which would support the ordination of women as not only permissible within Christianity but as a necessary corrective to a tradition of unjust exclusion. In answer to this, the declaration falls back, as we have seen, on the male physicality of Jesus and the fact that "[i]t is indeed evident that in human beings the difference of sex exercises an important influence, much deeper than, for example, ethnic difference."[22] But this is exactly the delicate compromise that Aristotle reached in considering the mystery of the difference between the sexes, with even the same specification that it is of importance primarily or exclusively "in human beings." That difference is neither essential, as between species, nor accidental, as between ethnic groups, but one of inferiority or defect of "matter" despite sameness of "form," or "intellectual nature." There seems to be no other way to make sense of this argument, all disclaimers to the contrary.

2

What options are available to those who would argue in favor of ordaining women? The four arguments McBrien lists divide into two rough groupings: arguments from the "human dignity" of women and arguments based on alternative interpretations of biblical texts and the practices of the early church. Similar categories appear in the commentaries that were published with the declaration in *Women Priests: A Catholic Commentary on the Vatican Declaration*. The first sort of argument is weakened by the fact that, in keeping with both Aristotle and the Gospels, the line of thought sketched out above denies neither the rationality of women nor the respect due them. Aquinas, like Aristotle, merely gives them second place. The declaration,

---

22. "Declaration," in *Women Priests,* ed. Swidler and Swidler, 45.

likewise, says that "the Church is a differentiated body, in which each individual has his or her role. The roles are distinct, and must not be confused; they do not favour the superiority of some vis-a-vis the others, nor do they provide an excuse for jealousy."[23] Women are in this way like those who lack the intellectual abilities needed for ordination and who may instead be welcomed into the nonordained brotherhood, as some initiates are welcomed by the Franciscans. Simply to reassert that women have "full human and Christian dignity,"[24] like the purported "right" of women to be ordained, does not constitute an argument against their exclusion from the priesthood. The question is precisely how the dignity of women, like the dignity of the intellectually challenged, is best served by the Catholic Church.

The second sort of arguments, which rely on a different interpretation of texts and the tradition, are similarly limited in their effectiveness by the fact that their opponents, like the author(s) of the declaration, may simply deny the meaning or relevance of the textual and historical evidence that they bring to bear. There is much debate, for instance, about whether Jesus called anyone to the ordained priesthood, as opposed to discipleship or the apostolate.[25] Among others, Rosemary Radford Ruether, in her contribution to the *Women Priests* volume, notes that there is a considerable gap of time separating the founding of the church and its institutionalization from "the elevation of the Christian ministry to the status of a sacred caste within the established Church of a Christianized Roman empire."[26] Elsewhere she also cites, with regard to the paradox already noted between the spiritual equality of women and their earthly subordination, the division some scholarship traces between early Christianity and what she calls "the Jesus movement."[27] The declaration, on the other hand, says that "a number of convergent indications . . . make it all the more remarkable that Jesus did not entrust the apostolic charge to women," but continues to maintain both that he unequivocally did not do so and that this in itself establishes the need to maintain an exclusively male

23. "Declaration," in *Women Priests,* ed. Swidler and Swidler, 47.
24. McBrien, *Catholicism,* 854.
25. McBrien, *Catholicism,* 853.
26. Rosemary Radford Ruether, "Women Priests and Church Tradition," in *Women Priests,* ed. Swidler and Swidler, 236.
27. Rosemary Radford Ruether, *Sexism and God-Talk: Toward a Feminist Theology* (Boston: Beacon Press, 1983), 195–96.

priesthood.[28] What seems clear is that contradiction, historical reconstruction, and alternative interpretations will not settle the matter as long as the church relies on "iconic representation" as its basic argument.[29]

Why might some people in the contemporary world believe that it is wrong for the Catholic Church not to ordain women? The fact that other Christian denominations do so is scarcely an argument, not only because those groups are by definition not part of the true church, but also because they do not carry in their history the same fidelity to tradition, and especially to the Thomistic tradition, with its ambivalent understanding of the status of women. Rather, they draw their basic metaphysical understandings from, and/or helped create them for, the Enlightenment. For this reason, I would disagree with Ruether's argument that the ordination of women in what she calls the "Western" (i.e., Protestant) churches is a break from the tradition of an exclusively male priesthood, because it is precisely not a break in the *Roman Catholic* tradition. On the other hand, the Anglican Church, which maintains the tradition of Apostolic succession, has largely adopted Enlightenment concepts of human equality and freedom, which render their historic reluctance to ordain women in some ways more problematic than the Roman Catholic tradition's absolute refusal. Similarly, Protestant denominations that arose more directly out of the Enlightenment—such as the Society of Friends, the early Methodist Church, and the Church of Christ—were also among the first to allow women to preach.

Despite the negative opinion of women's capabilities held by some of the most notable Enlightenment thinkers,[30] the theoretical generalization of Enlightenment tenets of equality and liberty to include women, as well as non-European men, began almost at once, even if it took a

---

28. "Declaration," in *Women Priests,* ed. Swidler and Swidler, 40.

29. The June 6, 1997, edition of the *National Catholic Reporter* contains an article that says, "The Vatican earlier this year backed off from its previous argument that the ban [on the ordination of women] is founded in scripture or tradition," relegating it to what the headline calls the "murky world of 'secondary truths'" that are necessary for "safeguarding the 'fabric of revelation.'" The article, which focused on the status of "secondary truths" and infallibility, gave no indication that either a full justification for the change or a revised statement of the argument against ordination had been given.

30. I am thinking here of Rousseau and Hume in addition to, obviously, Kant; Diderot and Voltaire were, perhaps, exceptions.

century or two for the message to take hold in the broader society.[31] This tradition denies the careful compromise Aristotle established in saying that the difference between men and women was neither essential, as is a difference in species, nor accidental, as is a difference of color, but one that lies in the "individualized matter" of each person.[32] Within the Enlightenment tradition, gender difference has come to be seen as accidental. This means that no one, not even one who most strongly opposes the ordination of women, is inclined these days to say that women are misbegotten men, but it remains the case that the deepest roots of the Catholic tradition rest on exactly that understanding of what it is to be human. The same antiquity of the tradition can be seen in the argument that McBrien cites to the effect that no one, male or female, has the "right" to be ordained,[33] even if he or she meets all the criteria listed above. Ordination is contingent, in a way more reminiscent of Plato's *Republic* than of Aristotle, on being judged to have the undeformed nature of Man, which found its fullest realization in Jesus. Rights and equality have no place in the conceptual world that underlies this practice.

If an objector cannot use rights and equality as the basis for supporting the ordination of women, however, she still need not accept that given the Catholic Church's unspoken but deep beliefs about the nature of women, they are justly excluded from the priesthood. Since the tradition itself is internally divided, there remains the option of placing one of its parts against the other, but this must be done hermeneutically, and not merely by appeals to other traditions, historical reconstructions, or a superficial reinterpretation of selected texts. The approach would be similar to that used in those evangelical movements that allowed women to preach based, not on Enlightenment ideas of equality, but on the testimony of the Gospels and Saint Paul that women were welcomed into Jesus' inner circle and preached in the early church. It would be necessary not merely to reinterpret the biblical texts under discussion but to do so with a clear commitment to the priority of the biblical message over the practices (and interpola-

---

31. See here, for example, Mary Wollstonecraft, and John Stuart and Harriet Taylor Mill. As should be clear from the earlier discussion of Kant, I am aware that this is a rather generous reading of the Enlightenment tradition on the questions of both gender and race, but a more detailed account would take the discussion too far from the immediate argument here.
32. Aristotle, *Metaphysics*, 218.
33. McBrien, *Catholicism*, 853.

tions) of the later, fully institutionalized church, and to find those resources in the Hebrew Bible that also support the spiritual and human equality of women. This must also be done with the clear aim of reevaluating the Thomistic legacy that would attempt to bridge the gap between doctrine and practice with an Aristotelian sleight of hand that seems to run contrary to the biblical tradition. Moreover, any change must come from within Catholicism to call the church away from errors inherited from pagan philosophy and back to the core message of Jesus' ministry and the earliest Christian churches.

This is not to minimize, of course, what a monumental transformation such a move would be for the Roman Catholic faith. The ordination of women is not like the liberalization of the rules for annulment through which the church has adjusted to another area of major change in modern life. A church cannot become merely more liberal about ordaining women—either it does or it doesn't. In this case, although not in as many others as people tend to think, the issue about women is almost precisely parallel to the issue about non-European men, that is, which differences are essential to the nature of a human being and which are accidental.[34] Opponents need, in short, to say clearly that women are not misbegotten men and, therefore, that they can also represent the "icon" of Jesus, and apparently did so in the early church. The Enlightenment presuppositions we take for granted in almost every other arena of contemporary life cannot be assumed in this case, because the tradition in question is far older, and far less flexible, than the merely political or social order. What is needed, instead, is not tendentious historical reconstructions of early Christianity, but a deep hermeneutical reading of the key texts that underlie the church's attitude toward women, as well as an investigation of the meaning of ordination itself. Only in this way can opponents even hope to convince those in power within the Roman Catholic Church that what they are doing, however ancient and well-founded on certain crucial texts, is deeply inappropriate in light of principles well founded on other, even more ancient and crucial texts.

---

34. Although the ordination of non-European men has never, to my knowledge, been an explicit issue in the Roman Catholic tradition, it is also the case that the ordination or elevation of non-European priests is often thought cause for a press release, and race has traditionally been an issue with regard to ordination in the Church of Jesus Christ of Latter-day Saints (Mormons), and less officially in some sects of American Protestantism.

How convenient, one might say, that my well-informed outsider's analysis of what is appropriate in this situation fits so well with the standard analysis based on Enlightenment values, and with my own clear prejudices. While I will gladly admit a certain reluctance to regard myself as inherently defective vis-a-vis men, I would also point out that the Enlightenment values themselves can, in part, be traced to the development of a Protestantism that grew out of a return to the message of the Gospels and a clear rejection of Thomistic philosophy. This development was not, of course, concerned directly with the status of women, but promoted a spiritual equality and liberty abstract enough that it could, in time, be applied "even" to women. It should be no surprise, then, that my critique of the Roman Catholic tradition in this area converges with those of many other thinkers who are explicitly pursuing their own sense of the appropriate. In other areas where I have attempted preliminary investigations along these same lines, for example, the moral acceptability of voluntary polygamy (including voluntary polyandry), my tentative conclusions may be less consoling to contemporary common sense. So much the worse, perhaps, for my conclusions, but at least this result gives some indication that the hermeneutic investigation of what is appropriate within a given tradition may be something more than the reiteration of the investigator's own prejudices. As Gadamer says, "A person who does not admit that he is dominated by prejudices will fail to see what manifests itself by their light."[35]

---

35. Gadamer, *Truth and Method*, 360.

3
The Appropriate Present

> After all, she is this Inappropriate/d Other who moves about with always at least two/four gestures: that of affirming "I am like you" while pointing insistently to the difference; and that of reminding "I am different" while unsettling every definition of otherness arrived at.
> —Trinh T. Minh-ha, introduction to *Discourse* 8, "She, the Inappropriate/d Other"

What follows is neither an objective nor a complete review of contemporary ethical theories. Rather, I have chosen theories and authors who function in the same general area of thought—postmodern ethics—and share many of the same assumptions as my own work. Virtue theory, for instance, traces its most basic concepts back to the work of Aristotle, but also shares my suspicion of traditional ethical discourse in a way that is not usually found in most contemporary deontological theories that stand in a similar relationship to Kant's work. Among the virtue theorists, I have chosen to focus on two of the most prominent, Alasdair MacIntyre and Martha Nussbaum, whose understandings of virtue theory also differ in interesting ways. Among the explicitly postmodern ethical theorists, I have chosen to discuss, again, the one who is undoubtedly best known, Richard Rorty, and the one whose work is equally undoubtedly the most like mine, Drucilla Cornell. The choice among feminist theorists working in ethics was much more difficult. Some women working in this area might not wish to be labeled feminist in the strong sense used here, and conversely, some women who are avowedly feminist might reject the imputation of "postmodernism." At the same time, one of the most interesting things about contemporary feminist ethical theory is the wide diversity of viewpoints it includes. For these reasons, I have chosen to focus on the work of two thinkers who represent voices that are avowedly feminist, arguably postmodern, and "other" to the voices heard here so far, legal theorist Patricia Williams and philosopher Claudia Card.

The Vices of Virtue Theory

One recurrent response to my efforts to teach Aristotle's *Nicomachean Ethics* is the valiant effort many undergraduates make (or made, until I began to warn them explicitly against it) to argue that some "minor" moral failing, for example, pilfering from an employer, would be acceptable to Aristotle, since those responsible are undoubtedly persons of good character and Aristotle believed that people should be judged by their characters, not their acts. Such students find his statement that the "man, however, who deviates little from goodness is not blamed, whether he do so in the direction of the more or of the less, but only the man who deviates more widely" (1109b), so unerringly that I have come to suspect that it is engraved on the wall of some Greek organization's men's room. (Of course, it also helps that it occurs early in the *Nicomachean Ethics*.) I know, of course, that this is a serious misuse of Aristotle's text, but my suspicion of so-called virtue theory in ethics may well have its roots there. At the same time, since such theories generally arise from the same awareness as my own of the need for a nonfoundational approach to ethics, since they also reject the possibility of a rule-based ethical theory formulated in terms of instrumental or scientific rationality, and since they turn to Aristotle's work in search of guidance for alternatives, these theories merit some serious consideration as rival approaches, as it were, to the one argued for here under the concept of appropriate action.

David Solomon offers a useful definition of what he calls "virtue ethics." He says that such a theory "will typically have three central goals":

1. to develop and defend some conception of the ideal person;
2. to develop and defend some list of virtues . . . ;
3. to defend some view of how persons can come to possess the appropriate virtues.[1]

Aristotle is the model of such a theorist because he offers a concept of the ideal person as happy, or blessed; develops from that concept a definition of virtue in general and lists of specific virtues; and tells us how to instill such virtues in our dependents and our fellow citizens. In similar ways, contemporary virtue theorists have responded to the postmodern moral crisis by defending an ethics that returns to the Aristotelian concepts of virtue and the good life, rather than isolated acts of harm or benevolence, as the basic units of analysis. Such theories, however, run the same three risks that plagued Aristotle himself: they can become relativistic, accepting whatever virtues may be present in a tradition at any given time or place as their starting point (this is Terence Irwin's claim about Aristotle's ethics as "weak dialectics"); they can transform merely local virtues into universal ones, based on a supposedly neutral concept of human nature (this is one of Sarah Broadie's concerns); and in either case they can remain uncritical of the actual virtues and practices current in their own culture or others they encounter—that is, they can be inherently conservative.

1

While Alasdair MacIntyre at times seems to want to argue against some forms of relativism, it is always in terms of a strong historical relativism. He argues that some cross-cultural judgments may be possible, in the same way that Kant argues for free will, by showing that the opposing view has unacceptable consequences: "But where there is no resort to such [neutral, independent] standards [of rational justification], human relationships are perforce relationships of will and power unmediated by rationality."[2] He underscores what is at issue by

---

1. David Solomon, "Internal Objections to Virtue Ethics," in *Midwest Studies in Philosophy, Volume XIII—Ethical Theory: Character and Virtue*, ed. Peter A. French, Theodore E. Uehling Jr., and Howard K. Wettstein (Notre Dame, Ind.: University of Notre Dame Press, 1988), 429.
2. Alasdair MacIntyre, "Relativism, Power, and Philosophy," in *After Philosophy: End or Transformation?* ed. Kenneth Baynes, James Bohman, and Thomas McCarthy (Cambridge, Mass.: MIT Press, 1987), 396.

setting the problem in terms of the Spanish conquest of the Zuni and the English conquest of Ireland. There are three steps to his argument that some sense may be made of a choice between these two ways of life potentially faced by bicultural participants in each. In the first step he argues that what such a bicultural person needs is some third language that would allow him or her impartially to investigate the advantages and disadvantages of both cultures, and that some modern language could serve that purpose. In the next, crucial step he explains that the modern language could do so only because it is itself so cut off from its own underlying beliefs and canons of meaning as to be "neutral" in the sense that it is neutered by its own diversity of moral traditions. Finally, he argues that we cannot stop at this point of analysis, but must "transcend" relativism.[3] He claims elsewhere that this can be done through a proper understanding of "Aristotle's fundamental moral scheme," which he believes has proved its superiority to competing value systems over time in the same way as a successful scientific paradigm.[4]

Such a reliance on Aristotle, however, because it is historicist, cannot offer a truly transcendental basis for judging any and all alternative traditions. In one place MacIntyre argues that "there are important transformations both in the concepts of particular virtues and in the concept of a virtue, so that although, for example, it may be true that in most, perhaps even in all social and cultural orders there is something which it is appropriate to name by our word 'justice' or by some relevantly cognate expression, it is not thereby true that one and the same quality or one and the same set of qualities is being accounted a virtue."[5] In the specific case of *sōphrosunē* he also wants to argue that its use in both Plato and Aristotle serves to undermine the traditional meanings found in Homer, claiming that for the later Greeks "genuine virtues are dysfunctional to any but the best form of life."[6] This critical use of the concept, however, must remain within the terms of ancient Greek culture and cannot depend on any transcendental meaning of

---

3. MacIntyre, "Relativism, Power, and Philosophy," 405.
4. Alasdair MacIntyre, "The Relationship of Philosophy to History," in *After Philosophy*, ed. Baynes, Bohman, and McCarthy, 419.
5. Alasdair MacIntyre, "*Sōphrosunē:* How a Virtue Can Become Socially Disruptive," in *Midwest Studies in Philosophy, Volume XIII*, ed. French, Uehling, and Wettstein, 1.
6. MacIntyre, "*Sōphrosunē*," 4.

the term that might be of use in contemporary life, since he also believes that "from an Aristotelian standpoint, it can never be right to weigh preferences in such a way that everybody counts for one and nobody for more than one," a view that MacIntyre goes on to characterize as an "absurdity."[7] He concludes that in a modern, highly diverse society, such as ours, Humean virtues, for example, may serve to question both the system in which they arise and the competing virtues represented by an Aquinian perspective on the world.

While MacIntyre's account of the process through which an Aristotelian concept of the virtues can serve a critical function within a particular cultural tradition is in many ways similar to my own, especially with regard to *sōphrosunē*, it is much more difficult to see how his account could be applied to moral judgments in genuinely cross-cultural situations. He seems oddly blind, in any case, to the power relations inherent in his own examples. One has to wonder what good our modern ability to see the comparative advantages and limitations of Zuni, Spanish, English, and Irish conceptual and moral schemata would be to an actual bicultural person caught several hundred years ago between these very different ways of life. By far the most common cases of biculturalism in both situations would be women taken, largely involuntarily, into the conquering cultures for sexual and other domestic uses. Their choice, then, to put it crudely, would be between being effectively enslaved whores in the new culture or traitorous whores in the old.[8] It is hard to see how a third language, such as modern English or French, to use MacIntyre's own examples, and the conceptual scheme it provided would do anything to mitigate the pain of what was undoubtedly most often a forced choice, or how an Aristotelian moral scheme would provide such victims of colonialism with any basis for either resistance or basic self-worth. The actual historical transition was made, of course, with the indirect help of Aristotle, through the medium of the church, but the way in which that was accomplished is not, I would think, an argument in favor of either the value or the neutral universality of his moral scheme.

7. MacIntyre, "*Sōphrosunē*," 6.
8. See Cheríe Moraga's "From a Long Line of Vendidas: Chicanas and Feminism," excerpted in *Feminist Frameworks,* ed. Alison M. Jaggar and Paula S. Rothenberg (New York: McGraw-Hill, 1993), 203–12 (from Moraga's *Loving in the War Years: Lo que nunca pasó por sus labios* [Boston: South End Press, 1983], 90–144).

2

On the other side of the coin, Martha Nussbaum chooses to avoid the risks of relativism and conservatism by embracing the second possibility, universalism. She faults relativistic versions of virtue theory as insufficiently Aristotelian, since Aristotle "was not only the defender of an ethical theory based on the virtues, but also the defender of a single objective account of human good, or human flourishing."[9] Her claim is based on the supposed "objective" universality of an ethics based on the virtues of Aristotle's time and place (as well as the correlated concept of "human flourishing" in terms of the courage, temperance, and so forth, of aristocratic men reliant on the wealth and leisure produced by slave labor), and the resultant ability critically to examine not only other systems of virtues and concepts of what constitutes "flourishing" (Christian ones, perhaps),[10] but also recalcitrant features of the culture from which they are derived: "And one of Aristotle's most obvious concerns is the criticism of existing moral traditions, in his own city and in others, as unjust or repressive, or in other ways incompatible with human flourishing."[11] Exactly how his concern to criticize unjust and repressive conditions is to be reconciled with Aristotle's acceptance of slavery and the segregation of women from public life is not made entirely clear.

Nussbaum's argument in this article is that Aristotle's virtues identify a definitive list of spheres of any possible life and then specify ideal human functioning in each. The minimal universalism here is that if the list is truly definitive, then anyone who disagrees with Aristotle about how to act in any particular area is still "arguing about the same thing, and advancing competing specifications of the same virtue."[12]

---

9. Martha Nussbaum, "Non-Relative Virtues: An Aristotelian Approach," in *Midwest Studies in Philosophy, Volume XIII,* ed. French, Uehling, and Wettstein, 33.

10. A Christian thinker at the Center for the American Experiment in Minneapolis has suggested that the Ten Commandments constitute "a moral code, essential for human flourishing," at least for Christians and Jews (Katherine Kersten, "Decline of Religion Is Central to the Malaise Afflicting America," *Star Tribune,* November 22, 1995, A15—she does not refer to the role of the Commandments in Islam), but it is hard to see how rules dictating that one should be monotheistic and keep a Sabbath while refraining from idolatry or swearing (40 percent of the Commandments) can be essential to "human flourishing" in any sense that would be acceptable to Aristotle, or perhaps even to Nussbaum.

11. Nussbaum, "Non-Relative Virtues," 33.

12. Nussbaum, "Non-Relative Virtues," 36.

She then considers several objections that might be raised by a persistent relativist. To begin with, although Aristotle defines the situation so that we are arguing about the same things, it is not clear that we will ever agree on a single answer. More seriously, it is not clear that the spheres of human life she finds in Aristotle are in fact definitive of any possible way of life.[13] Her first response to such challenges is that Aristotle might be able to accept a disjunctive virtue, a limited list of "contenders" for the best way to live in that sphere, a list that might be enriched by contextual factors as well.[14] In fact, she wants to make being sensitive to the social context of one's actions an "absolutely, objectively" right thing to do (whatever Christian missionaries might have thought),[15] although she also wants to produce a list of "areas of greater universality" of moral concern, based on what is necessary to human flourishing.[16]

Nussbaum does not make clear, however, what the grounds might be for overriding local sensitivities in a social context that accepts what we would consider unnecessary human pain (an area of "greater universality") when the justification for such practices relies on a claim that they actually foster human flourishing. Female genital mutilation, for example, is sometimes justified on the basis that it frees women from the temptations of illicit sexuality so they might be better wives and mothers, and it is not clear how Nussbaum could counter such an argument, though surely she would disagree with it. It is, in any case, clear that she can have no argument to counter the Catholic Church's refusal to ordain women, since ordination seems not to be essential to the sort of flourishing that interests her (although the same is probably not true for Aristotle).

Criticism of positions such as Nussbaum's come from many directions. Nancy Sherman believes that Aristotle himself might reject the idea that any one list of primary moral concerns could be universally determined in advance. "[T]he actual placement and overall fit of goods in an integrated life is the task of practical reason and *nous;* it is the task, that is, of ethical perception, emotional sensitivity, and choice. It cannot be done in the abstract."[17] In times of famine, for instance, the

---

13. Nussbaum, "Non-Relative Virtues," 40.
14. Nussbaum, "Non-Relative Virtues," 43–44.
15. Nussbaum, "Non-Relative Virtues," 45.
16. Nussbaum, "Non-Relative Virtues," 48–49.
17. Nancy Sherman, "Common Sense and Uncommon Virtue," in *Midwest Studies in Philosophy, Volume XIII,* ed. French, Uehling, and Wettstein, 108.

flourishing of adult bodies might be secondary to the survival and healthy development of infant and child bodies, and food appropriately distributed accordingly. This is *not* to say that everything possible must not be done to avoid such situations, but only to say that one cannot decide in the abstract and in advance that all mothers who choose to feed their children before themselves are deluded to see some value in their choice. On this view, Nussbaum, and by extension any universalist-leaning virtue theorist, has paid insufficient attention to Aristotle's own sensitivity to context, one that rules out the possibility of prejudgment of any sort.

David Solomon lists both "external" and "internal" objections to virtue theory as he defines it. Among the latter are those that have already been mentioned, including what he calls the "action-guiding objection," that is, the fact that reliance on the virtues in ethical thought "lacks the capacity to yield suitably determinate action guides."[18] Solomon argues that virtue theorists tend to defend their position against such charges by proving, first, that an appeal to virtue has more content than the objection admits and, second, that their primary rivals, utilitarianism and Kantian deontology, offer less concrete content than the objection assumes. In both cases, the problem is that virtues are not, and were never meant to be, guides to specific acts; they are guides to ways of life that have clear implications for how to act in particular cases. (This is the point that my students miss.) Solomon himself seems to be willing to gain more concrete guidance from the virtues by recourse to what he calls a "local teleology," a move that would place him, along with MacIntyre, in the relativists' camp.[19]

Many virtue theorists are reluctant to cast either Aristotle or themselves as moral conservatives, but are uncertain whether relativism or universalism is the greater danger. The former leaves us in the ethically uncomfortable position of having no rational basis to decide between Aristotelian and Christian virtues, the Zuni and the Spanish, utilitarian Humean and monkish Aquinian ways of life, as MacIntyre puts it, although we might be able to use the one to correct the excesses of the other (as perhaps Aquinas did with Christianity and Aristotle). The second leaves us in the epistemologically uncomfortable position

---

18. Solomon, "Internal Objections," 432.
19. Solomon, "Internal Objections," 434.

of developing a value-free concept of "human flourishing" that will accommodate both our own intuitions and Aristotle's list of virtues. My starting point has been that there is no metaphysical position outside of any given tradition, no transcendental foundation from which to develop such a concept. Perhaps even in extreme famine all food should be divided equally among everyone. I would certainly want to think that all adults, at least, should be given equal shares. Having lived all my life in the United States, however, the postcolonial world presents me with too many reasons to question my ability to judge fairly for me even to consider that I might be as wise about such things as those immediately involved. A far better guide seems to me to be provided by a hermeneutic interpretation of what the deepest traditions of the culture in question determines to be appropriate, when viewed through a critical understanding of *sophrosune* and practical wisdom as defined in that culture.

The Limit of Philosophy

Rather than a definition of postmodern ethics, here I will offer only genealogies (in the traditional sense) to relate the views discussed to my own. For instance, of the ethical theories discussed in this chapter, the one that may sound the most like the position I am arguing for is found in Richard Rorty's *Contingency, Irony, and Solidarity*. This is not a contingency. My undergraduate training in philosophy was heavily influenced by the pragmatism of the prewar generation of professors who retired soon after my graduation, to be replaced by the properly analytic/linguistic philosophers who now tread those hallowed sandstone arcades. It was not until graduate school that I encountered large doses of "mainstream" Anglo-American philosophy, and then in the form of the ordinary language philosophy on which Rorty also draws. More important, in graduate school I studied the work of Heidegger and Derrida with Hubert Dreyfus, who has also worked closely with Rorty. Thus, it was no surprise finally to turn to Rorty's book and find that we have few, if any, major disagreements about either contingency or irony, although he is perhaps more skeptical of theory than I. (We might have slightly larger disagreements about the best way to read Heidegger or Derrida, but that is another issue.) Where we disagree is with regard to solidarity, and especially the adequacy of the idea that "cruelty is the worst thing we do" as the primary concept in moral thought.[20]

1

Rorty's historical perspective is much the same as my own, although he would not want to make the distinction I do between the apparently foundational moral theories of Plato and Mill and the all but overtly nonfoundational theories of Aristotle and Kant. He says of all moral principles alike that they "only have a point insofar as they incorporate tacit reference to a whole range of institutions, practices, and vocabularies of moral and political deliberation. They are reminders of, abbreviations for, such practices, not justifications for such practices."[21] He also sees the critical use that can be made of ironic "alienation" within a given cultural tradition, suggesting that "the poet and the revolutionary are protesting in the name of the society itself against those aspects of the society which are unfaithful to its own self-image."[22] His goal, moreover, is much like mine (give or take the word "liberal): "In what follows I shall be trying to reformulate the hopes of liberal society in a nonrationalist and nonuniversalist way."[23] Rorty believes that we can revive these hopes by becoming what he calls "liberal ironists," committed to an awareness of the contingency of our most basic beliefs and to a human solidarity based on decreasing the cruelty humans do to each other. At the same time, there are hints that his conclusions are not going to be entirely satisfactory. First, there seems to be a lingering universalism, if not ethnocentrism, hiding in the bottom of Rorty's irony basket. Second, and more important, avoiding cruelty seems an inadequate solution to the moral problems central to the present discussion.

The first such hint is Rorty's surprising acceptance of Freudian theory, scarcely an example of how to maintain the contingency of one's

---

20. Rorty borrows the phrase from Judith Shklar. See Richard Rorty, *Contingency, Irony, and Solidarity* (New York: Cambridge University Press, 1989), xv.
21. Rorty, *Contingency, Irony, and Solidarity*, 59.
22. Rorty, *Contingency, Irony, and Solidarity*, 60. (Clearly, having been on a university campus during the late 1960s is another formative experience that Rorty and I share.)
23. Rorty, *Contingency, Irony, and Solidarity*, 44–45.

historical situation. Rorty summarizes Freud's view as a case of "seeing every human being as consciously or unconsciously acting out an idiosyncratic fantasy," something he describes as "distinctively human."[24] What is this, if not an account of how human beings "must" be, that is, of human nature? He seems to believe that Western social and political theory need go no farther than Mill's libertarianism,[25] but makes it no clearer how such a claim is compatible with his rejection of any possible "final vocabulary." Even more disconcerting is his later claim that "liberal irony" is *only* possible for contemporary enlightened persons like ourselves: "The ironist does not see her ability to envisage, and desire to prevent, the actual and possible humiliation of others—despite difference of sex, race, tribe, and final vocabulary—as more real or central or 'essentially human' than any other part of herself. Indeed, she regards it as an ability and a desire which, like the ability to formulate differential equations, arose rather late in the history of humanity and is still a rather local phenomenon."[26] Apparently Jesus and the Buddha just didn't have a chance to be truly enlightened, living in the morally backward times and places they did. Only now can lucky Westerners be "liberal."

Rorty would, perhaps, tell us to do as he says, not as he does. The question remains, however, whether what he says will be enough to deal with the moral problems we face. He relies on the diminution of cruelty as a single ethical dictate, at the same time admitting, as of course he must, that "[t]here is no *neutral*, noncircular way to defend the liberal's claim that cruelty is the worst thing we do."[27] He also admits that Nietzsche, at least, would disagree. More relevant, however, is the indeterminacy of the term "cruelty" itself. Many of those who practice the genital mutilation of girls would probably consider it a far greater cruelty to condemn them to life as unmarried women than to perform the clitoridectomy needed to make them acceptable wives, and it is not at all clear that Rorty could disagree. The only reasonable basis for such disagreement would have to involve some notion of cruelty that could be related back to the virtue theorists' concept of "human flourishing." Rorty, however, has barred himself

---

24. Rorty, *Contingency, Irony, and Solidarity,* 36
25. Rorty, *Contingency, Irony, and Solidarity,* 63.
26. Rorty, *Contingency, Irony, and Solidarity,* 93.
27. Rorty, *Contingency, Irony, and Solidarity,* 197, emphasis in the original.

from that avenue by saying of Hilary Putnam's reliance on such a concept that "the root of scientism, defined as the view that rationality is a matter of applying criteria, is the desire for objectivity, the hope that what Putnam [and Nussbaum] call 'human flourishing' has a transhistorical nature."[28] Since he goes on to equate such scientism to the positing of gods, he clearly would reject any attempt to ground his own concept of cruelty in anything other than what might be considered cruel, or more cruel, within a given tradition. Ironically, of course, he would have to accept the Catholic Church's refusal to ordain women, since this would not amount to cruelty on any construal of the situation with which he would possibly agree, since its importance to the women involved relies on an even stronger metaphysical belief in "gods."

Another reason he is forced into this position is that he wishes to resurrect in a new form the public/private distinction that many feminists hoped had been put to rest long ago. On Rorty's view, self-creation is a personal, private issue, the realm of Marcel Proust, Nietzsche, Heidegger, and Derrida. The public realm of liberty, on the other hand, is represented by Charles Dickens, Mill, Jurgen Habermas, and John Rawls. Such a distinction serves his purpose well, since he wants to agree with all of these thinkers despite the divergence of their views, but he goes on to assert that the public realm has no "*automatic* priority" over the private.[29] While concerned with private cruelty, he leaves it to literature to exercise moral authority over it. One cannot help wondering, however, whether Vladimir Nabokov's intricate condemnation of the cruelty inherent in Humbert Humbert's depriving Lolita of her childhood would carry much moral weight within a tradition where child brides were the norm. When governments and public opinion alike support a private cruelty as central to some important social institution, it is not entirely clear how literary authority alone could keep the cruelty from happening. (*Uncle Tom's Cabin* is, perhaps, the exception that proves this rule.)

Even in less extreme cases, Rorty seems rather insensitive to the cruelties that can exist within the private realm. He says at one point that the "only important political distinction [with regard to moral

---

28. Richard Rorty, "Solidarity or Objectivity?" in *Anti-Theory in Ethics and Moral Conservativism*, ed. Stanley G. Clarke and Evan Simpson (Albany: State University of New York Press, 1989), 174.

29. Rorty, *Contingency, Irony, and Solidarity*, 194, emphasis in the original.

opinions] is that between the use of force and the use of persuasion." There seem to be large areas of gray, even in the public realm, between force and persuasion. When we are talking about the private sphere, the room for cruel persuasion is even wider. What recourse would Rorty's "liberal ironist" have in such a situation? Solidarity seems an inadequate starting point, especially as long as "our sense of solidarity is strongest when those with whom solidarity is expressed are thought of as 'one of us,' where 'us' means something smaller and more local than the human race." This may be an unavoidable empirical fact, but what I find strange is Rorty's apparent endorsement of it, and apparent casualness about its negative import: "My position entails that feelings of solidarity are necessarily a matter of which similarities and dissimilarities strike us as salient."[30] He would make more similarities and fewer dissimilarities salient in our attempts to eliminate cruelty, but my position would suggest that this is, in fact, a *reductio* of his attempt to base any kind of ethical conclusion on the mere concept of solidarity. If a concept of appropriate action relative to specific cultural practices could serve instead as a nonfoundational basis for a critical moral understanding, it would seem a better way to draw the moral conclusions that Rorty and I would both want to draw.

In fact, it is not clear in many cases that relying on solidarity and the avoidance of cruelty will allow us to draw any particular conclusions at all. The situation that confronts the Madwoman and her friends, for instance, does not suggest any obvious solution in terms of cruelty, or if it does, it would be to spare the minions of modernity rather than condemn them. Part of the point of their "trial" is to establish that they are not "us" and so to allow their eradication. Moreover, the scene of their actual dispatch to the sewers of Paris is presented in a dreamlike fashion meant to weaken, it could be argued, our sense of their demise as an act of "cruelty."[31] Disagreeing with the Madwoman's reasons, or the intuitions Giraudoux evoked in providing them, would not be a concern for Rorty, since he takes the demand that ethical rules "make room" for moral intuitions to be a "reactionary slogan."[32] He might have the same reaction to the concept of the appropriate itself, since

---

30. Rorty, *Contingency, Irony, and Solidarity*, 84, 191, and 192.
31. Jean Giraudoux, *The Madwoman of Chaillot*, adapted by Maurice Valency (New York: Dramatists Play Service, 1947), 60–64.
32. Rorty, *Contingency, Irony, and Solidarity*, 21.

he says later that "appropriateness is a matter of taking up a place within a preestablished and familiar pattern."[33] So, there is a real possibility that, for Rorty, the Madwoman and her friends are wrong, that they lack a sufficient sense of solidarity with the President and those he represents, who should be encouraged through the morality embedded in literature (such as *The Madwoman of Chaillot*, perhaps) to cease their cruelty to their fellow human beings. And if in the meantime they raze Paris to drill oil wells, *tant pis,* one supposes. It is hard to reconcile any form of environmentalism with Rorty's exclusive moral concern with cruelty.

As suggested above, however, "cruelty" might offer less protection even for vulnerable humans than does a concept of appropriate action. My position would not only accept the Madwoman's reason, leave the public/private distinction open to negotiation depending on local circumstances, and avoid equivocation about what constitutes "cruelty" (arguing about what is "appropriate" would at least focus on texts rather than persons), but it would not require even the minimal concepts of human nature that Rorty borrows from Freud and Mill. It requires only the faith, if you will, that all traditions have some basic beliefs that could be used critically to evaluate current practices that seem problematic to some of those within the tradition or to well-informed outsiders. It would also be more consistent with any feminism that might wish to deny that "recognition of a common susceptibility to humiliation is the *only* social bond that is needed"[34] (e.g., because some feminists might believe families also provide necessary social bonds). At the same time, this approach would maintain the contingency and irony of Rorty's claim that "[w]e can keep the notion of 'morality' just insofar as we can cease to think of morality as the voice of the divine part of ourselves and instead think of it as the voice of ourselves as members of a community, speakers of a common language."[35] What it also would reject would be his further claim that solidarity alone can provide an adequate language for morality, even of a "liberal ironist" sort—assuming a liberal ironist might care about the environment and accept the Madwoman's reason.

---

33. Rorty, *Contingency, Irony, and Solidarity,* 160–61n.
34. Rorty, *Contingency, Irony, and Solidarity,* 91, emphasis in original.
35. Rorty, *Contingency, Irony, and Solidarity,* 59.

2

Drucilla Cornell and I have little shared "genealogy," but what we do have is crucial: we share the firm belief that Derrida's work is both profoundly ethical and intrinsically feminist. In *The Philosophy of the Limit*, however, Cornell traces Derrida's work back in quite different directions than I do, not to Heidegger but to the texts of Immanuel Levinas, Jacques Lacan, Theodor Adorno, and ultimately to Hegel. As a lawyer, she also writes within a different intellectual context, so that her interlocutors are not Aristotle and Kant, but political theorists such as Rawls and Habermas, members of the critical legal-studies movement, and justices of the Supreme Court. Her attempt to provide us with a "'new' ethical configuration"[36] is, therefore, more complex than my own. Her primary objective is to redefine Derrida's "deconstruction" as the "philosophy of the limit" in order to make its ethical import clear.[37] This redefinition is based on the fact that the deconstruction of a specific text (or institution) reveals the way in which that text is related to the Other that exceeds it, that is, to its own limits. In Chapter 1, for example, we saw how Derrida's "deconstruction" of Heidegger's use of words related to the concept of the appropriate pointed beyond the modern understanding of the terms to an Other represented by a premodern way of relating to property and to oneself. Aristotle would seem, on my reading, to be the last rem(a)inder available to us of an entirely Other relationship to what is one's own, a delimitation of the modern.

Thus, in some sense, Cornell's response to Derrida is the converse of my own. Where I would argue for the ethical use of the concept of the appropriate, with an admitted implicit reference to the self in the modern world, Cornell chooses instead to privilege the relationship to the Other in her ethical and legal thought. Despite her deep differences with Rorty, this emphasis on the Other seems to echo his singular focus on cruelty, as when she defines the "ethical relation" in terms of "the kind of person one must become in order to develop a nonviolative relationship to the Other."[38] Again, I have tried to reappropriate a

---

36. Drucilla Cornell, *The Philosophy of the Limit* (New York: Routledge, 1992), 9.
37. Cornell, *Philosophy of the Limit*, 155.
38. Cornell, *Philosophy of the Limit*, 13.

social concept of appropriate action, as a critical understanding of the deeply shared values of a particular tradition, whereas Cornell points out that, for Adorno, one of the Others that is of concern is that material Other which is my own body, my own pleasure. The shared insight behind these seemingly opposite moves is, I would venture, the opposition they both maintain with ethics as either a rational, rule-based decision process centered on the "ought" or a repetition of community practices centered on the "is." That is, we are both, in our own ways, pointing to the limits of traditional moral thought in an attempt to create an ethics that will not violate our sense of ourselves as both female and moral persons by either forcing us into male-defined modes of ethical thought or trapping us in the existing realm of patriarchal convention. As Cornell points out, when the "observer" is a woman, the limits of existing systems of moral, legal, and political thought take on a different shape.[39]

Cornell's argument has two positive goals. The first is to argue for the deeply ethical significance of Derrida's work, despite his own reservations about "ethics" as usually understood. This is necessary because of the widespread opinion that Derrida's work is morally and politically nihilistic, which she traces to the silence Derrida believes must be maintained in the face of the forgotten Other as a moral force. "It is precisely the silence before the name of the prescriptive or ethical force heeded in the philosophy of the limit that has misled many readers to argue that what has been called deconstruction has to do with the radical indeterminacy of meaning and, therefore, with the impossibility of ethical judgment."[40] Cornell notes instead the opening represented by this silence, the invitation it offers "to think again."[41] In this way, her concerns agree with my own emphasis on the critical use of the concept of the appropriate, or the call of the Other, in evaluating traditional moral thought. At the same time, however, this rethinking is not a random process of someone's doing with the text "what he would," because, she points out, we are rethinking "something," reading some text. In a rare reference to Heidegger, she adds that the

39. Cornell, *Philosophy of the Limit*, 144.
40. Cornell, *Philosophy of the Limit*, 63.
41. Cornell, *Philosophy of the Limit*, 71. For a fuller discussion of the controversy about the ethical and political implications of Derrida's thought in a feminist context, see Nancy J. Holland, ed., *Feminist Interpretations of Derrida* (University Park: Pennsylvania State University Press, 1997).

"ethics of reading practiced by 'deconstruction' commands us to heed 'things.' "[42] She regards Derrida's reluctance to address ethics head-on as a tendency to radicalize Heidegger's own skepticism about its metaphysical basis in humanism.[43] Her use of Levinas, and others, is an attempt to supplement Derrida's own silence.

Cornell's second positive goal is to apply the conclusions she draws regarding ethics to issues in current legal theory. Because the law just is the codification of a society's central moral beliefs, her ideas here are even closer to my own. She offers a theory of legal interpretation that is meant to maintain a balance between the Good (i.e., some determinate, if unrealizable, concept of the Good Life), the Right (i.e., some equally unrealizable Kantian standard of correct action), and any given existing legal system by a "double gesture" of acknowledging both the impossibility of reconciling them and the necessity of doing justice, which is defined precisely as such a reconciliation. The Good is defined as "the universals within a given legal system conceptualized as an indeterminate *nomos*," that is, as the deepest, but often unarticulated, beliefs underlying a culture's specific legal practices. The reference to the Good here as a critical tool, then, could be understood as the need for particular legal decisions or particular laws to be, in my terms, appropriate within the terms of that *nomos*. She maintains that in reclaiming a concept of the Good in legal thought, "what is rejected is not the ideals of modernity, and certainly not the 'gains' of a modern legal system, but instead the illusion that a normative conception of modernity can be so self-grounding that the realm of the Good is at best irrelevant and at worst a regression to the premodern."[44] The premodern, all that is the Other of the modern, she suggests, still has a place in the law.

The Good, or the *nomos*, provides Cornell with what she calls legal principles (as opposed to legal rules) that could serve as "lighthouses" of justice.[45] These principles would not be universals that tell us the path we must follow to achieve justice, but rather warning signals of

42. Cornell, *Philosophy of the Limit*, 81–82.
43. Cornell, *Philosophy of the Limit*, 82.
44. Cornell, *Philosophy of the Limit*, 92.
45. The figure of lighthouses appears in the original article from which this section of *Philosophy of the Limit* was derived. See Drucilla Cornell, "From the Lighthouse: The Promise of Redemption and the Possibility of Legal Interpretation," *Cardozo Law Review* 11, nos. 5–6 (1990): 1687–714.

what we must avoid. Such principles could provide a basis outside the existing law for interpreting that law in terms other than its own, but at the same time would not themselves have any fully independent existence in some other realm, because Derrida teaches us there can be nothing outside of a particular cultural or legal system on which it can ultimately be grounded or based. There can be no "appeal to 'external' norms to legitimate the system. Nor, on the other hand, does he argue that the system can only appeal to *internal* norms, as if there could be a rigid distinction between the internal and the external."[46] One specific dimension in which the principles generated by the Good would work within our current legal system, Cornell suggests, would be in the realm of gender relations. She uses the psychoanalysis of Jacques Lacan, radicalized through Derrida, to expose the patriarchal, indeed, phallogocentric underside of our culture and the ways in which it serves to counter the interests of women in our legal practices. Our principle of equality, for instance, is severely undermined by the hierarchical way in which gender is necessarily understood in our culture. A legal or political use of Derrida's work allows us to see, Cornell argues, that "[g]ender hierarchy is thus not only false, it is unethical."[47]

Cornell also offers careful criticisms of alternative views. For my purposes here, the most interesting of these are her critique of communitarianism and her rejection of Rorty's work. Her primary complaint against communitarian moral and legal thinking, not surprisingly, is that it is too conservative, especially with regard to gender issues.[48] Given her definition of the communitarian perspective as one that "would have us rely on the embodied, concrete norms of our actual communities to guide us in our legal and political commitments and disputes," she does acknowledge the importance of such a focus on community in the thought of both Derrida and Adorno, but goes on to point out that "twentieth-century experience has presumably taught us that the appeal to community ineluctably slides into an appeal to totality, closure, and exclusion."[49] The criticism of this position amounts to more than a simple gesture toward recent (and current)

---

46. Cornell, *Philosophy of the Limit*, 142, emphasis in original.
47. Cornell, *Philosophy of the Limit*, 175.
48. For a similar feminist critique of communitarianism, see Lorraine Code's *What Can She Know?* (Ithaca, N.Y.: Cornell University Press, 1991), 276–77.
49. Cornell, *Philosophy of the Limit*, 6, 37, and 39.

history, however. Part of the impact of Derrida's work has been to establish that "there can be no self-enclosed tradition, ethical or otherwise, which will not show the effects of the economy of *differance*."[50] That is, the concrete beliefs of any given tradition will always already be open to what is Other to that tradition, the practices of Roman Catholicism, for instance, to an Aristotelianism grounded in pre-Christian Greece. This creates the critical power of the appeal to principle (or a sense of the appropriate). To the extent that communitarians rely on an illusory "pure" or artificially purified tradition, they risk violating basic principles, or acting inappropriately.

Cornell clearly considers Rorty's views to be a elaborate form of conventionalism or relativism that shares many of the problems she finds in communitarian views. She groups him with Gadamer as a "pragmatic Hegelian," criticizing both as insufficiently sensitive to the inequalities of power hidden within the appeal to solidarity, to "the relations of domination and exclusion which are implicated in an abstract appeal to the 'we' who *share*."[51] As I argued above, this insensitivity to the vulnerability of the internal Other has a special significance with regard to power relations within the family and what might constitute either "solidarity" or "cruelty" in intimate relationships. She argues later that Derrida explicitly denies "the move we now associate with the recent versions of 'pragmatism.' The 'conversation of mankind,' for Derrida, does not do away with the Other to us as 'material' reality."[52] One reason she gives for this is that any appeal to "rational" conversation can easily disguise a male-defined concept of reason itself.[53] Another part of the reason for the rejection of "pragmatism" is that, for Cornell, "justice can never be reduced to the conventions of the 'is,' "[54] but always demands the double gesture toward an impossible justice for the Other. Moreover, since Cornell shares my sense that there is a deep ethical imperative in Derrida's work, we also reject the claim made by Rorty, and others, that postmodernism necessarily implies ethical nihilism. Cornell puts it more strongly:

---

50. Cornell, *Philosophy of the Limit*, 56.
51. Cornell, *Philosophy of the Limit*, 35, emphasis in original.
52. Cornell, *Philosophy of the Limit*, 178, footnote reference to *Contingency, Irony and Solidarity* omitted.
53. Cornell, *Philosophy of the Limit*, 203 n. 51. On this point, see also my *Is Women's Philosophy Possible?* (Savage, Md.: Rowman & Littlefield, 1990).
54. Cornell, *Philosophy of the Limit*, 181.

"[T]he identification of deconstruction with ethical skepticism is a serious misinterpretation."[55]

So, where does the substance of Cornell's views differ from those presented here under the concept of the appropriate? I believe that the difference is simply the one between ethics and the law. In any legal system there are principles that can serve as lighthouses to guide it away from the dangers recognized within the tradition of which it is a part. One could even argue that the principles represented by current Western concepts of human rights have a certain claim to providing lighthouses that might be applicable in other traditions, or at least to codifying them in a more effective way. But a concern with the Good Life, with *sophrosune,* seems not so easily transferable from one tradition to another without damage to the integrity of each system. Law can be argued to have a common purpose in all its possible contexts—to resolve conflict in such a way that the society remains intact. As with cooking, another practice with a universal goal, some things just work better for that purpose than do others, so that ignoring the rule that laws, not men, should govern, for example, can be seen as analogous to using dirty utensils. Visions of the Good, however, vary far too much in their purposes across cultural contexts to generate even minimal substantive standards. We have already seen how an appeal to rights fails in the arguments around the ordination of women in a Catholic tradition that draws on pre-Enlightenment concepts of the Good. That is why I have offered a concept of appropriate action as a "formal" standard, something analogous to the material limits on the production of textiles, despite the widely diverse roles they play in different cultural traditions.[56] If a legal system aims toward the Good, that Good must be Other to that legal system and to the substantive aims embodied in it.

In practice, this means that I am not clear where Cornell's way of thinking would lead us with regard to the Madwoman's reason. As an example of legal adjudication, the "trial" of the President and his cohort fails many simple tests of justice, either by French or American standards. Despite the Madwoman's many efforts to be fair, the mere fact that the defendant is represented by a partisan of the other side

---

55. Cornell, *Philosophy of the Limit,* 100.

56. For a fuller development of this argument with regard to the use of the concept of the appropriate in epistemology, see my "Theory/Practice Distinction Shows Up in Practice: Some Thoughts on Epistemology and the Law," *European Journal of Law, Philosophy, and Computer Science* 1–1 (1998):1 49–57.

turns the whole thing into farce, which is, of course, the point. Cornell might also note, as pointed out above, how Giraudoux dehumanizes those the Madwoman condemns exactly at the point of the execution of the judgment against them. I suspect that, like Rorty, she would prefer to see the point of the play to be one of converting people like these from ravagers of the social and physical environment to positive forces of change, since she also shares his concern with the moral importance of literature. But we cheer for the Madwoman, and Giraudoux's text coerces us into doing so. Is he just revealing the hidden Nazi inside each of us? I think not. Rather, the inclusion of a "trial" within the play might serve to draw exactly the distinction I am relying on here, that between what is permissible in the legal realm and what we may find morally desirable or at least morally acceptable. "I *am* the law," says the President, and the audience realizes at once that this is not enough. Not that Cornell would say that it was, but her concern with the law allows her to draw stronger substantive conclusions than can be drawn in the ethics without the danger of cross-cultural insensitivity.

The Feminist Other

Both Drucilla Cornell and I would consider ourselves to be feminists. In choosing feminist alternatives to my own ideas about the use of the concept of the appropriate in ethical thought, therefore, I looked for theorists whose views, while in some ways similar to my own, might arise from different life experiences, as well as different conceptual backgrounds. In using the term "feminist ethics," I relied on the definition that Rosemarie Tong borrows from Alison Jaggar: "No matter what else an approach to ethics does or does not do, in order to be 'feminist' it must (1) proceed on the assumption that women and men do not share precisely the same situation in life; (2) offer action guides 'that will tend to subvert rather than reinforce the present systematic subordination of women'; (3) provide strategies for dealing with issues that arise in private or domestic life; and (4) 'take the moral experience of all women seriously, though not, of course, uncritically.' "[57] These

---

57. Rosemarie Tong, *Feminine and Feminist Ethics* (Belmont, Calif.: Wadsworth, 1993), 164. The two quoted passages are from Alison M. Jaggar, "Feminist Ethics,"

criteria suggest a rather interesting classification of the authors discussed above, since it seems to allow us to group Nussbaum with Cornell, despite the otherwise extreme difference in their views. Thus "feminism" is not a monolithic ethical position, but at the same time not just anything counts.

Before beginning my discussion, it might be best to acknowledge that the "feminist" ethics with which many philosophers are most familiar these days is derived from the work of Carol Gilligan and her associates. This research seems to show that women have what is called a "care" orientation in making moral decisions, based on their life experiences as both daughters and mothers, while men have the "justice" orientation that is reflected in most mainstream ethical thought. The conclusion Gilligan draws is that our understanding of moral reasoning should be broadened to include both "care" and "justice" orientations. She does not, however, consider the more politically salient conclusions either that the "care" orientation reflects women's status as oppressed persons or that the "justice" orientation might be part and parcel of that oppression. Thus, Tong herself classifies Gilligan's work as "feminine" rather than "feminist" ethics because she believes that feminist ethics requires a more political approach.[58] My concern with Gilligan's work is that it separates out the "care" orientation as a feature of women's moral reasoning, thus accepting "justice" as the norm, instead of investigating the historical and cultural specificity of the "justice" orientation itself.[59] These feminist reservations about Gilligan's work have led me to bypass it here, despite its popularity, in favor of the work of two thinkers who might better provide a feminist "Other" to both traditional ethical theory and the strictly postmodern discourse out of which Cornell's work and my own arise.

---

in *Encyclopedia of Ethics,* ed. Lawrence Becker, with Charlotte Becker (New York: Garland, 1992), 366–67.

58. Tong, *Feminine and Feminist Ethics,* 158–61. Both Tong and Claudia Card offer thorough critiques of "feminine" ethics. See also Tong, *Feminine and Feminist Ethics,* 220–26, and Card, *Lesbian Choices* (New York: Columbia University Press, 1995), 76–78.

59. On this point, see my "Opinions of Women and Men: Toward a Different Configuration of Moral Voices," *Journal of Social Philosophy* 24, no. 1 (1993): 65–80.

1

As with Cornell, the fact that Patricia Williams is a law professor and legal theorist does not mean that her work has no implications for ethics. In fact, the very form of her writing carries an ethical message —"subject position is everything in my analysis of law"—because she believes the supposed impersonality of legal discourse serves to conceal the power relations in the law and to promote oppression. "[T]he myth of a purely objective perspective, the godlike image of generalized, legitimating others—these are too often reified in law as 'impersonal' rules and 'neutral' principles, presumed to be inanimate, unemotional, unbiased, unmanipulated, and higher than ourselves." This myth, she says later, is not itself neutral but is meant "to empower still further; to empower beyond the self, by appealing to neutral, shared, even universal understanding."[60] Of course, this "ruse" of objectivity is found in many fields besides the law. Williams sees her attempt to develop an "ambivalent, multivalent way of seeing" in the law as also "at the core of what is called critical theory, feminist theory, and much of the minority critique of the law."[61] As opposed to a legal positivism that puts too much faith in the decontextualized written word, and a legal realism that, along with feminist and traditional civil rights theories, suggests a "me too" approach to the legal status quo, she wants to affirm what I would call a postmodern interpretative stance that "is not 'nihilism' but a challenge to contextualize, because it empowers community standards and the democratization of interpretation."[62]

Seen from this perspective, Williams's project is much like my own. She "would like to write in a way that reveals the intersubjectivity of legal constructions, that forces the reader both to participate in the construction of meaning and to be conscious of the process."[63] She also sees many of the same problems in the "theoretical legal understanding" that have already been discussed in philosophy: the reification of oppositional categories; the reliance on "transcendent, acontextual, universal" truths, with a corresponding disparagement of the historical, contextual, and specific; and the ruse, referred to above, of "unme-

---

60. Patricia Williams, *The Alchemy of Race and Rights: Diary of a Law Professor* (Cambridge, Mass.: Harvard University Press, 1991), 3, 11, and 92.
61. Williams, *The Alchemy of Race and Rights,* 130.
62. Williams, *The Alchemy of Race and Rights,* 109.
63. Williams, *The Alchemy of Race and Rights,* 7–8.

diated voices."[64] Her purpose is to reexamine "what is lost by narrow interpretative ideologies, and of rediscovering those injuries made invisible by the bounds of legal discourse."[65] The Madwoman represents a moment when we are persuaded to see that in just this time at just this place for just these people an action seems morally right, even morally necessary, but could be given no justification under any existing system of ethical rules or judicial interpretation. Williams's continuing concern for the homeless she encounters in her life resonates, for me at least, with Giraudoux's vagabonds, just as Cornell's characterization of Derrida's method resonates with Giraudoux's Ragpicker. At the same time, however, as already noted, such insights may carry different weight in ethical discourse, of however diffuse a form, than they do in the law.

Williams thus agrees with Cornell, as opposed to the critical legal studies movement, that it is much too soon to surrender the notion of human rights. While Cornell gives a primarily pragmatic argument for the continuing need for these legal "lighthouses," Williams provides a highly contextualized argument based in African-American history and life experience. She argues that "[a]lthough rights may not be ends in themselves, rights rhetoric has been and continues to be an effective form of discourse for blacks," and suggests that, instead of abandoning rights language, we "attempt to become multilingual in the semantics of evaluating rights."[66] In her discussion, she focuses both on the fact that those in critical legal studies have "qualitatively different experiences of rights" than her own and on the claim that arguments about the preferability of legal discourse couched in terms of needs "overlook a long history of legislation *against* the self-described needs of black people."[67] Her conclusion is that "[f]or blacks, then, the battle is not deconstructing rights, in a world of no rights; nor of constructing statements of need, in a world of abundantly apparent need. Rather the goal is to find a political mechanism that can confront the *denial* of need. The argument that rights are disutile, even harmful, trivializes this aspect of black experience specifically, as well as that of any person or group whose vulnerability has been truly protected by rights."[68]

64. Williams, *The Alchemy of Race and Rights*, 8–9.
65. Williams, *The Alchemy of Race and Rights*, 110.
66. Williams, *The Alchemy of Race and Rights*, 149.
67. Williams, *The Alchemy of Race and Rights*, 150–51, emphasis in the original.
68. Williams, *The Alchemy of Race and Rights*, 152, emphasis in the original.

The advantages that Williams's argument on this point might have over Cornell's—its specific grounding in life experience and the forceful clarity of her writing—mark it as both profoundly feminist in Tong's sense of the term and as an argument that functions primarily within the American legal system. While Williams's characterization of the reasons behind the rejection of the concept of human rights may be correct, the same reconsideration of their ultimate usefulness can be based in the problems of cross-cultural moral evaluation that I have been emphasizing here. As I argued above with regard to Cornell, it is much less clear in ethics than in the law that any "neutral" standards such as human rights can be invoked by Western observers in other cultural contexts without at least an a priori risk of cross-cultural insensitivity. Given her concern with context and her rejection of "universal," disembodied discourse, Williams would possibly agree. While rights are insufficient to guarantee women the right to ordination in the Catholic Church, some defenses of female genital mutilation, even in the United States, are formulated in terms of the right to freedom of religion or the right of a family to raise their children as they see fit. In those contexts, rights language can do harm, and any full moral theory must account for how and why that is the case. As a lawyer, however, what Williams gives us is a clear, convincing argument for the perpetuation and evolution of rights language in the American judicial context, but not something that she probably never intended to give—a theory of ethics that could be applied across cultures and across time.

2

As with Williams's discussion of "race and rights," most of the moral problems Claudia Card considers in *Lesbian Choices* involve specific ethical dilemmas, in this case those faced in lesbian, gay, and feminist communities. At the same time, her thinking on these issues seems implicitly to reflect the position, espoused by many postmodern thinkers, that we can have moral rules, but not moral principles. Tong defines this distinction as follows: "Whereas moral principles apply in any and all circumstances, moral rules apply only to recurring specific situations."[69] That is, the solutions Card suggests to the moral dilem-

---

69. Tong, *Feminine and Feminist Ethics*, 14. Note that for Cornell these terms are reversed with regard to legal rules (determinate universal dictates) and her

mas she considers tend to be closely tied to concrete contexts and circumstances. Thus her discussion of "horizontal violence" in the lesbian community may not be generalizable to communities where, for instance, ostracizing a perpetrator is not a viable option (although Card rejects it for lesbians as well) or where appeal to the legal system carries fewer dangers, for both the individual and the community. Similarly, the conclusions she draws about the ban on gays and lesbians in the military and about "outing" may not translate directly into other situations. She says explicitly that "[i]n lesbian ethics, that assumption [of eternal, universal truth] is replaced by leaving open questions of wider applicability for others to answer for themselves."[70]

The question with which she begins echoes one preoccupation here, the cross-cultural applicability of key philosophical terms. Card makes it clear that this is really two problems: "The logical problem is whether it makes *sense* to apply the term 'lesbian' outside its cultural home. The ethical problem, presupposing the intelligibility of such usage, is whether doing so is disrespectful."[71] She solves the problem quite ingeniously by suggesting a definition of "lesbian" in terms of three paradigms (amazonian, sapphic, and "passionate friends") related by what she calls a Wittgensteinian family resemblance and reinforced by a Nietzschean genealogy.[72] Her concern with cross-cultural validity is also reflected in her choice of the term "particularistic" for her work, rather than either "universal" or "relativistic," a distinction she defines by saying, "Relativism denies the existence of universally . . . valid norms or values. Particularist ethics need not deny such possibilities, but neither does it take as its objective the articulation of ethical norms or values in abstraction from the kinds of particulars that differentiate some groups of people from others. Like universalist ethics, it aims for truth, or better, for truths."[73] Thus, her work is "revolutionary in relation to philosophical traditions of Western European thought," reflecting a skepticism she shares with most feminist philosophy about "rules and rights, institutions, hierarchies, dualisms,

---

own "lighthouses" of legal principles, as discussed above. In law the equivalent of "moral rules" as defined here would probably be specific legal decisions.
   70. Card, *Lesbian Choices,* 74.
   71. Card, *Lesbian Choices,* 16, emphasis in the original.
   72. Card, *Lesbian Choices,* 30–32.
   73. Card, *Lesbian Choices,* 74.

and competition."⁷⁴ This would, as I suggested, also make her work arguably postmodern.⁷⁵

The one possible exception to the "particularism" of Card's approach is her insistence on justice as a determining value. This arises in the context of her consideration of Sarah Lucia Hoagland's *Lesbian Ethics*, where Hoagland "questions not only the primacy but the value of the concept of justice for contemporary lesbian communities."⁷⁶ Instead, Hoagland wants to focus on what is needed to "elicit and enhance agency and integrity" in lesbians, where "*attending* is a major strategy of empowerment."⁷⁷ Card raises the possibility that not all attending is "friendly," and suggests, analogously, that not all control is bad, especially "controls that we may need for self-defense."⁷⁸ Later, Card specifically reintroduces the concept of justice, for reasons that call to mind the point Williams makes about rights, based on the life experience of a particular community: "I remain skeptical of rejecting justice while injustice is so prevalent in our interactions with one another. If justice has not helped us, that may be because we have been excluded from its institutions, discouraged from using them, and discouraged from learning to perceive injustice against ourselves. . . . Instead of hastening to abandon the idea of justice, we might appreciate more fully how little justice we have known."⁷⁹ To the extent, however, that justice is defined universally, either in terms of law or of Aristotelian virtue, it is not clear that it would retain its helpful aspects in all possible cultural situations, something that Card would no doubt acknowledge.

What of the Madwoman, or perhaps, in this context, of the madwomen? By what one could call a sort of serendipity, although it might only reflect the depth and breadth of certain stereotypes, the other three madwomen in Giraudoux's play correspond roughly to Card's three paradigms of lesbianism: Constance, the Madwoman of Passy, to the sapphic; Gabrielle, the Madwoman of St. Sulpice, to the "passion-

---

74. Card, *Lesbian Choices*, 73.
75. For one version of this "argument," see Sara Ahmed, "Beyond Humanism and Postmodernism: Theorizing a Feminist Practice," *Hypatia* 11, no. 2 (1996): 71–93.
76. Card, *Lesbian Choices*, 73.
77. Card, *Lesbian Choices*, 125, emphasis in the original.
78. Card, *Lesbian Choices*, 126.
79. Card, *Lesbian Choices*, 146.

ate friends"; and Josephine, the Madwoman of La Concorde, to the amazonian. Does this constitute anything more than a parody of a lesbian community? Giraudoux makes it clear that this is a group of older women closely bound together by ties of affection, shared experience, common values, and many years of "attending" to each other, in Hoagland's sense of the term. As such, they serve as prosecutors and judges, on the French model, for the trial of the minions of modernity. Moreover, the voices they raise are most often women's voices: Constance, who has been momentarily charmed by the Ragpicker's portrayal of the President, quickly changes sides when he brags that because of his wealth women fall for him "like tin cans from a second-story window," to which she says, "This is going a little far, I must say."[80] The judgment that they render, along with the vagabonds, can be seen as reflecting a particularistic moral rule, specific to this situation, that leaves open its applicability to others for those others to decide for themselves. But to say this says nothing about how this decision, and the reason for it, might be correlated to other decisions of a similarly complex and extralegal nature in a different cultural or social context; it is not to give a general reason.

The attentive reader will have noticed at this point that I have not yet made any argument that the use I am suggesting here for the concept of appropriate action is itself a kind of feminist ethics. To the extent that feminist ethics, as illustrated in the cases of Williams and Card, seems to focus on moral rules rather than moral principles and on the particular rather than the abstract, such a claim has a *prima facie* implausibility. Card asks "why ethics?"[81] but the question here would seem to be "why ethical theory?" Why do feminists need more than moral rules? I would argue that some sort of ethical theory is needed if we are to speak intelligibly about the moral value of actions and practices in significantly different moral contexts. The particularism of Williams, Card, and others, while making their work rich and accessible in the American context, suggests little about what one might do, or must do, in radically unusual, unrulelike cases such as that which faces the Madwoman, or in cases where the cultural context is radically different. Would it be unjust to deny fathers the right to submit

---

80. Giraudoux, *The Madwoman of Chaillot*, 56.
81. Card, *Lesbian Choices*, 58.

their daughters to clitoridectomy? Such an argument could certainly be made, however one defines justice or rights. It could *not* be made on the basis of a feminist moral stance, of course, but then the issue becomes whether feminist ethics are as invidiously particularistic as the "masculinist" ethics they are meant to replace. Why is the feminist stance in this case to be preferred?

While I would agree with Williams, Card, and the others that there is no eternal, universal answer to that question, I would suggest that the best way to go about determining the answer in any specific cultural context is to look, not at what is currently said, believed, and done in that culture, but at what is most appropriate in terms of the deepest moral values reflected in its concept of moral wisdom, *phronēsis* guided by *sōphrosunē*. If such an approach begins with the understanding that women's situation in life is not the same as men's, works to subvert the current gender hierarchy, applies to private as well as public life, and gives special attention to women's moral experience and insights in its critical evaluation of the practices within their own tradition, it would seem to be as feminist as any.[82] Giraudoux shows us how neither the Ragpicker nor any of the other men in his play could do what the Madwoman does, although she could not do it without their help. Just as it must be Hector and Ulysses who try so hard to stop the Trojan War in *Tiger at the Gates,* it is vital that a woman, a Madwoman, speaks for Giraudoux in this situation. What can be said, even by a man, only in a woman's voice would seem necessarily to be feminist in at least some significant sense. Here it is not the voice of an abstract Other, but rather that of the stereotypical Other of the instrumental reason embodied in the modernity that he seeks to combat. "Nothing is ever so wrong in this world," the Madwoman says, "that a sensible woman can't set it right in the course of an afternoon." [83] Unfortunately, she is mad.

---

82. Compare the criteria already cited from Tong, *Feminine and Feminist Ethics,* 164.
83. Giraudoux, *The Madwoman of Chaillot,* 66.

Conclusion

The Appropriate Future

There is something even more *unheimlich,* eerier, about an introduction to a conclusion than about the conclusion to an introduction.[1] In the latter case, one is making a transition to the body of the work in question, but the work itself would seem to be a transition to the conclusion. What more could be needed? Perhaps a reminder of what remains to be resolved from the previous discussion, or at least that part of what remains unresolved that I hope to be able to bring to some resolution here. Two of the unresolved issues are closely related—the question, why moral theory? which arose in Chapter 3, and the place in my argument of the one ethical thinker I find both extremely interesting and somehow outside the present discussion, David Hume. I rely on the work of Annette Baier to bring these two problems together. The other topic that seems unresolved is the relationship between

---

1. On this general problem, see Jacques Derrida, "Outworks," in *Dissemination,* trans. Barbara Johnson (Chicago: University of Chicago Press, 1981), 1–59.

the theory developed here and related problems in other philosophical fields, such as aesthetics. Therefore, I will also return in more detail to the discussion of appropriate moral action in terms of the Heideggerian "ready-to-hand" and related concepts that was begun in Chapter 1, in an effort to draw on his more global philosophical enterprise at least to hint at how the concept of the appropriate might work in other realms of thought as well. While these final points will undoubtedly leave many other questions unresolved, it will in any case allow me to conclude the present conversation.

The Appropriate Moral Theory?

I started graduate school six years after receiving my bachelor of arts degree, with the intention of becoming a specialist in the work of David Hume. Fate intervened in the form of a course on Heidegger I took on a lark in my first year, but when Barry Stroud noted the similarity between a brief explanation of Derrida I gave at the end of my graduate career and Hume's philosophical position, I felt a certain sense of gratification. Thus it was that Hume played a major role in my first published book,[2] and in researching that topic I became familiar with Annette Baier's work. In developing the argument here, I felt a sense of gratification, much like that I experienced at my mock job interview many years ago, in reading her claim that "Hume's manifesto is a call for a self-critical, nonintellectualist, and socially responsible moral philosophy."[3] Needless to say, that is how I would describe my present endeavor, with only two minor qualms. The first would be that while I share Baier's and Hume's reservations about what is currently called moral theory, as indicated in the last chapter, I do believe that something else that might *also* be called moral theory remains important. Closely related to this is my second qualm: as already indicated, I have many concerns about the cultural relativism of Hume's moral position. At the same time, however, those concerns might not apply to a more

---

2. Nancy J. Holland, *Is Women's Philosophy Possible?* (Savage, Md.: Rowman & Littlefield, 1990).
3. Annette Baier, "Doing Without Moral Theory?" in *Anti-Theory in Ethics and Moral Conservatism,* ed. Stanley G. Clarke and Evan Simpson (Albany: State University of New York Press, 1989), 40.

fully developed version of that position. As Baier points out, there is still much work to be done in this area: "As I see it, it is not so much that Hume failed [to provide an alternative basis for ethics] as that his successors failed to continue in his project."[4]

Baier's definition of a moral, or normative, theory is "a system of moral principles in which the less general are derived from the more general."[5] Using this definition, she divides up the great names in philosophy along different lines than I have, grouping Aristotle with Hume as not providing a normative theory in this sense and Kant with Aquinas as doing so. Assuming that the general argument of Chapter 2 is correct, however, Kant's position would shift into line with Aristotle's and Hume's because the relationship of derivation to which Baier refers fails in his case as much as in Aristotle's, despite his manifest intentions. Assuming, moreover, that the general argument of this book as a whole has been made well enough, my intentions are clearly not to do theory in that sense, although I do believe in at least the possibility (if not the practical necessity) of an ethical theory formulated in terms of the concept of appropriate moral action, an ethical theory consistent with the view that "it remains mere prejudice to demand explicitness, universality, and coercive backing, in any moral guide. For any such guide to be passed on it must be learnable, but one can learn from example. For any such guide to be of general use, its precepts must apply fairly generally, but generality is not universality. For any such guide to be accepted *as* a guide, there must be some motive to accept it. But the motive need not be the avoidance of sanctions."[6] I would suggest that this is, in fact, a description of *sophrosune* in the wide sense the term has been used here.

The argument has been that, at the deepest level, moral theory cannot "demand explicitness, universality, and coercive backing," because those features are part of the "present-to-hand," in Heidegger's terms, of moral deliberation. These features of moral thinking only appear under certain unusual circumstances, collective or individual, where the usual "background" conditions of "ready-to-hand" ethical decision making no longer apply and our immediate responses to the ethically "unready-to-hand" fail to fit the situation. One important oc-

---

4. Baier, "Doing Without Moral Theory?" 37–38.
5. Baier, "Doing Without Moral Theory?" 33.
6. Baier, "Doing Without Moral Theory?" 37.

casion where such a breakdown of ready-to-hand moral rules fell into an unready-to-hand need for higher-level, critical thinking and from there into the present-to-hand moral rules derived from metaphysical theories was in ancient Athens, and Alasdair MacIntyre argues that a critical use of the concept of *sōphrosunē* played an important role in that transition.[7] Even in the tradition that grew out of that particular set of historical contingencies, however, the project of making every aspect of our moral lives explicit, universal, and logically dependent on some transcendent metaphysical reality has had limited success. After the end of metaphysics, we understand why that had to be the case. Clearly the solution is neither to look for other present-to-hand rules (e.g., the economic ones to which Baier refers)[8] to guide our moral actions, nor to fall back on some communitarian set of unexamined ready-to-hand rules limited to a specific cultural and historical context. Rather, we might look at the moment of moral breakdown, the moment of the unready-to-hand, as a guide to a future "minimal" moral theory.

The sudden unreadiness-to-hand of our usual ways of ethical decision making occurs in two paradigmatic cases: unusual moral problems within a particular cultural tradition and situations of cross-cultural moral conflict—hence the Madwoman's reason as a privileged example and the genital mutilation of girls as a fixed limit of thought here. The problem that faces the Madwoman cannot be dealt with in any ready-to-hand way, because it is of a scope and a nature that go beyond ordinary moral choice. Her present-at-hand attempt to deal with the President and the others through an explicit legal process only establishes that they cannot be combated at that level, because the law also is part of the present-at-hand logic of modernity. She is thus left to rely on her own *sōphrosunē,* on her own sense of what needs to be done in the face of an unexpected ethical problem, which she exercised *before* the trial in her conversation with the Sewer Man. The verdict reached by the vagabonds and the other madwomen serves to confirm her sense of what is appropriate to do in this situation, but does not, cannot, decide the issue. We have also seen that moral theory, as usually understood, cannot give the Madwoman a

---

7. Alasdair MacIntyre, "*Sōphrosunē:* How a Virtue Can Become Socially Disruptive," in *Midwest Studies in Philosophy, Volume XIII—Ethical Theory: Character and Virtue,* ed. Peter A. French, Theodore E. Uehling Jr., and Howard K. Wettstein (Notre Dame, Ind.: University of Notre Dame Press, 1988), 1–11.

8. Baier, "Doing Without Moral Theory?" 36.

reason to do what she does. Her reason cannot be found in any preexisting, ready-to-hand moral rule or in present-to-hand principles, but only in what is appropriate to the particular context of the moral problem she faces. For us to understand her reason outside a direct experience of the play, however, requires something more, something like a theory or formal structure that allows us access to the unready-to-hand reason behind her reason.

That is why I would take exception to Baier's rejection of moral theory, as well as to any absolute commitment to the particularism invoked by Patricia Williams and Claudia Card. Within the American, and perhaps the wider European, context, we still need the concepts of rights and justice, as they and Drucilla Cornell argue, to protect those least able to protect themselves in the current distribution of power. In a postcolonial context, appeals to physical human flourishing, as Martha Nussbaum suggests, or to the avoidance of cruelty, as Richard Rorty suggests, might be more effective within specific contexts in which the meaning of those terms could be reasonably determined. All four sorts of arguments could be used to protect girls from genital mutilation in a given tradition, but none alone would guarantee such protection in the absence of the kind of power to enforce our values on others that seems in itself to be morally problematic. If we are to stop an obvious evil, as a practical matter, it can only be done from within each particular cultural context in which it occurs, based on the careful study of what is deepest and most important in the self-understanding of that tradition. To say that we will not, in such a hermeneutical approach, encounter any tradition that relies on the denial of justice and flourishing to some of its own members, or that relies on what we would call cruelty, may be an item of faith, but it seems to be a minimal one. This is also something we can only come to know through a moral theory based on the concept of appropriate action that provides a formal basis of evaluation across and between different specific traditions.[9]

---

9. On this, see Kwasi Wiredu's interesting comments on his reevaluation of the significance of actual Akan practices with regard to slavery and gender injustice in his postscript to *Cultural Universals and Particulars: An African Perspective* (Bloomington: Indiana University Press, 1996), especially 201.

The Art of Ethics

Invoking Heidegger's concept of the morally unready-to-hand as an occasion for the exercise of *sophrosune* allows us to relate the ethical concept of the appropriate to the larger structure of his work in order to illustrate in another way the relationship between theory and nontheory that is at work here. In *The Basic Problems of Phenomenology,* something of a companion piece to *Being and Time,* Heidegger explains the role of the unready-to-hand in a hermeneutical understanding of truth and being in ways that illuminate its more general role in his thought. He is clearest about this role with regard to epistemology, where he is making an explicit contrast between his position and "the usual approach in theory of knowledge."[10] His claim is that in coming to know the world, we do not first encounter random collections of decontextualized objects, but familiar items of use, the ready-to-hand. We only become aware of this "handy," to use Albert Hofstadter's translation of the term, when it fails to be handy, that is, when it becomes the "unavailable," or unready-to-hand. The relevant point here, however, is that this unavailability of the unready-to-hand occurs only on a background of the ready-to-hand and so conceptually belongs to the same realm of being: "*[H]andiness* and *unavailability* are specific *variations of a single basic phenomenon.*"[11] Even when the unavailable is annihilated, its nonexistence is not, he suggests, the same as nonbeing or nothing. One might think, instead, that its nonexistence is a variant form of its being as being-unavailable.

Why think that? Because, in the earlier discussion of truth, Heidegger makes a similar connection between *aletheia* as what is revealed and as what remains concealed—"Uncoveredness, truth, unveils an entity precisely as that which it already was beforehand regardless of its uncoveredness and non-uncoveredness"—where the foil of this argument is again philosophical and scientific knowledge.[12] Since truth is defined in terms of this uncoveredness, it is always relative to the possibility of being uncovered, that is, to the existence of Dasein in

---

10. Martin Heidegger, *The Basic Problems of Phenomenology,* trans. Albert Hofstadter (Bloomington: Indiana University Press, 1982), 304.
11. Heidegger, *Basic Problems of Phenomenology,* 305, emphasis in the original.
12. Heidegger, *Basic Problems of Phenomenology,* 220.

general, but *not* to the particular conditions under which it is factically uncovered, that is, a particular human culture. In both of these cases, being and truth, an apparently three-part structure can be reconfigured into a complex dualism. Things can be in truth as revealed or as concealed. Equipment can exist for us as handy or as unhandy, and are both to be distinguished from the merely present-at-hand. What is interesting here is the possibility of seeing works of art, such as *The Madwoman of Chaillot,* as themselves in some sense "unhandy," as on one side of, and grouped with, the usefulness of equipment, where the bare, present-at-hand thing would be opposed to both.[13] On this reading, the structural resonance between the unhandy and the work of art is reflected in the way in which works such as the great Greek tragedies or the photographs of Robert Mapplethorpe provide a third paradigm case of how we can encounter what is morally "unavailable," that is, how they reveal new moral dimensions of our world.

This account is similar to the way in which Hubert Dreyfus has used the analysis of "expert systems" (which he developed from a Heideggerian understanding of our everyday acting in the world) in his discussion of moral decision making and so-called moral "experts."[14] He has linked his work in this area with Carol Gilligan's discussions of a "care" orientation in ethical thought, but I believe the two issues can be separated because Dreyfus's primary concern is to avoid present-at-hand, rule-based theories and Gilligan's work is neither the only nor necessarily the best of the available alternatives to traditional ethical thought. The "expert-systems" approach would say that mature moral thinkers can solve most moral problems without significant explicit thought about what they are doing, just as chess masters respond to most of the moves on a chess board. When that process breaks down, when the appropriate move or moral response is "unready-to-hand," they must expressly think through the situation, or at least its most

---

13. This seems to be what Heidegger is working toward in the section of "The Origin of the Work of Art" entitled "Thing and Work," although I doubt that he would put it so explicitly. See his *Poetry, Language, Thought,* trans. Albert Hofstadter (New York: Harper, 1975), especially 29. It also seems to be implicit in Joan Stambaugh's translation of the "ready-to-hand" as "human artifacts," which would include both equipment and works of art. See Martin Heidegger, *On Time and Being,* trans. Joan Stambaugh (New York: Harper, 1972), 7.

14. Hubert L. Dreyfus and Stuart E. Dreyfus, "What Is Morality? A Phenomenological Account of the Development of Ethical Expertise," in *Universalism vs. Communitarianism,* ed. David Rasmussen (Cambridge, Mass.: MIT Press, 1990).

salient aspects. This is when chess games become slow. The problem that Dreyfus found in artificial "expert systems" is that they tend to address the more difficult problems in terms of present-to-hand rules and logic, which is not how experts in fact solve them. In these cases, and arguably in ethically problematic situations as well, the move from unready-to-hand to present-at-hand works against "expert" thinking. Works of art such as Giraudoux's *Madwoman,* Euripides' *Medea,* or Mapplethorpe's photography illuminate the morally unready-to-hand in a way that shows the inadequacy of explicit, "logical" moral theories to capture or justify an appropriate response.[15]

Both Aristotle and Kant see art as having a moral purpose, but also as in some sense extramoral. Aristotle defines tragedy as "the imitation of a good action, which is complete and of a certain length ... ; through pity and fear it achieves the catharsis of such emotions."[16] Since action is central, he sees tragedy as driven by plot, rather than character, and specifically by the plot devices of reversal and recognition. The tragic character must be neither completely good nor completely bad, so that the misfortune he falls into is seen as fearful or pitiful, that is, so that the audience can identify with his fate and those who hear the story will "shudder and feel pity even without seeing the play."[17] The manipulation of emotion, therefore, is the main focus of the poet's art, which is why Aristotle finds tragedy superior to epic poetry, because tragedy better achieves its "appropriate" pleasure.[18] Catharsis of the emotions of fear and pity, however, relies on the disproportion between the hero's tragic error and the fate that befalls him —it must be a terrible fate, not a proportionate or just one. Aristotle specifically cites as defective plots in which someone receives what he deserves.[19] Thus art reveals to us situations that exceed the strictly

---

15. My colleague Duane Cady is currently working on a project that would link moral and aesthetic judgment, based on the work of Suzanne Langer and Iris Murdoch. His work and my own clearly touch in many areas, and overlap in not a few, as should come as no surprise after an association of more than fifteen years.

16. Aristotle, *Poetics,* in *Aristotle on Poetry and Style,* trans. G.M.A. Grube (Indianapolis: Bobbs-Merrill, 1958), 12 (1449b), translation slightly modified.

17. Aristotle, *Poetics,* 27 (1453b).

18. Aristotle, *Poetics,* 62 (1462b).

19. Aristotle, *Poetics,* 38–39 (1456a). Hans-Georg Gadamer also notes that "the excess of tragic consequences is characteristic of the essence of tragedy" (*Truth and Method,* 2d ed., trans. Joel Weinsheimer and Donald G. Marshall [New York: Crossroad Press, 1989], 131).

ethical, but engages our emotional responses in such a way, presumably, as not only to cause us "its own peculiar kind" of pleasure,[20] but also to make us better people just by exposing us to dimensions of the moral that lie outside our normal experience.

The sublime in Kant works in much the same way both to teach us about the moral law and to illuminate what must exceed it. Moreover, while Kant speaks of the sublime primarily in terms of the natural world, he adds the proviso that he does so "since the sublime in art is always confined to the conditions that [art] must meet to be in harmony with nature."[21] Whereas beauty, for Kant, corresponds to the concepts of the understanding and is therefore within the realm of the knowable, although it is itself indeterminate, the sublime corresponds to the ideas of reason, "which, though they cannot be exhibited adequately, are aroused and called to mind by this very inadequacy, which can be exhibited in sensibility."[22] That is, the sublime cannot exhibit the ideas of reason adequately, not even in an indeterminate fashion, but the manifest fact that it cannot serves to direct the mind toward those ideas just because they are also unknowable, that is, because they cannot be adequately expressed or exhibited in any way whatsoever. As noted above, duty and freedom, being purely noumenal, remain completely empty ideas, and it is the utter incomprehensibility of the sublime that best represents that emptiness. As in Aristotle, for whom tragedy was moral in part because it still carried vestiges of the religious festivals in which it originated, in Kant the experience of the sublime in art appears in decontextualized religious sites: St. Peter's in Rome and the Egyptian pyramids. In both cases, what seems to be intended is not that the sublime reflect the divine, but rather that the divine suggest the extramoral reality art gives us.

Still, the ultimate manifestations of the sublime are, of course, religion and death. Jacques Derrida comes to this topic twice at least—once through works of art, in *Memoirs of the Blind*,[23] and once through what he characterizes as an explicitly Christian discourse, in *The Gift*

---

20. Aristotle, *Poetics*, 27 (1453b).
21. Immanuel Kant, *Critique of Judgment*, trans. Werner S. Pluhar (Indianapolis: Hackett, 1987), 98, bracketed word in original.
22. Kant, *Critique of Judgment*, 99.
23. Jacques Derrida, *Memoirs of the Blind: The Self-Portrait and Other Ruins*, trans. Pascale-Anne Brault and Michael Naas (Chicago: University of Chicago Press, 1993).

of Death,²⁴ which takes as its point of departure one of the essays in Jan Patocka's *Heretical Essays on the Philosophy of History* but also discusses in some detail Søren Kierkegaard's *Fear and Trembling*. Skirting the specifically religious, Derrida argues that moral responsibility is a paradox because it both requires knowledge of what one is doing (in a tradition that goes back, of course, to Aristotle) and asserts that one never really fully knows what one is doing, because, if one did, making a moral decision would be simply "the technical deployment of a cognitive apparatus."²⁵ That is, if one had the necessary present-at-hand knowledge to make a moral decision, it would no longer be a choice but a logical conclusion or a technical fact. Moral choice must fall within a realm that exceeds the ethical understood in terms of rules and algorithms, that is, in the realm of the unready-to-hand. As in Kierkegaard's discussion of Abraham and Isaac, "a decision is, in the end, always secret,"²⁶ because its reasons cannot be given in terms of publicly available rules. Thus what Derrida seems to offer us here is a moral metatheory, a way of generalizing Kierkegaard's arguments against the specific form moral theory takes in Hegel, so that it would provide something that might be the conditions for the possibility of an ethical theory.

Derrida does this by playing on the ambiguity of the Other in both Kierkegaard and Immanuel Levinas to remind us of the other of the Other, all those others who must be ignored in answering the call of one specific Other, theological or not. "If every human is wholly other, if everyone else, or every other one, is every bit other, then one can no longer distinguish between a claimed generality [that is, universality] of ethics that would need to be sacrificed in sacrifice, and the faith that turns towards God alone, as wholly other, turning away from human duty."²⁷ Thus the contrast that Kierkegaard wants to make between the publicness of the ethical and the secrecy of the religious sphere fails. What the Madwoman does is public, and publicly understood, but not for all that part of the Hegelian ethics of universal reason. It is also not "aesthetic," in Kierkegaard's sense, or subjective, but intersub-

---

24. Jacques Derrida, *The Gift of Death*, trans. David Willis (Chicago: University of Chicago Press, 1995).
25. Derrida, *The Gift of Death*, 24.
26. Derrida, *The Gift of Death*, 77.
27. Derrida, *The Gift of Death*, 84. For my interpolation, see the translator's footnote, 60n.

jective and particular in the sense used by Card. The only secret is the one the Madwoman shares with the Sewer Man, a secret Derrida allows for by noting that "[l]iterature concerning the secret is almost always organized around scenes and intrigues that deal with figures of death."[28] If Derrida gives us a metatheory for any future ethics of the appropriate, the Madwoman gives us one way in which it might be understood in our ordinary moral understanding of the extramoral. What I hope to have offered is the theory that lies in between, always mindful that the President and his clones are not given the gift of death (nor are they "disappeared")—they disappear voluntarily out of their own intemperate greed.

What is clear at the least is that Jean Giraudoux shares Heidegger's and Derrida's concerns about the direction and pace of change in the modern world. Heidegger says, "Perhaps there is a thinking which is more sober than the irresistible race of rationalization and the sweeping character of cybernetics. Perhaps it is precisely this sweeping quality which is extremely irrational."[29] This is no simple condemnation of modernity, but rather the suggestion that it has overstepped its limits. I have argued here that this is clearly the case with contemporary ethical thought, which tends to fall into either a deontological or consequentialist (pseudo)technology of moral decision making or a communitarian or postmodern relativism. The two sorts of response are not unrelated. As Heidegger tells us, "[T]he theories of relativism and skepticism spring from a partially justified opposition to an absurd absolutism and dogmatism of the concept of truth."[30] Nihilism and relativism are also, Nussbaum, Cornell, Williams, and Card remind us, dangerous for those in subordinate social positions. What I have tried to do here is to create some possibility for something beyond nihilism that would not be simply a return to "absolutism and dogmatism." That said, it is time to move on. As the Madwoman says, "Good. . . . Four o'clock. My poor cats must be starved. What a bore for them if humanity had to be saved every afternoon. They don't think much of it as it is."[31]

28. Derrida, *The Gift of Death,* 10n.
29. Heidegger, *On Time and Being,* 72.
30. Heidegger, *Basic Problems of Phenomenology,* 222.
31. Jean Giraudoux, *The Madwoman of Chaillot,* adapted by Maurice Valency (New York: Dramatists Play Service, 1947), 66.

Bibliography

Ahmed, Sara. "Beyond Humanism and Postmodernism: Theorizing a Feminist Practice." *Hypatia* 11, no. 2 (1996): 71–93.
Allison, Henry E. *Kant's Theory of Freedom*. New York: Cambridge University Press, 1990.
Aristotle. *Metaphysics*. Trans. Richard Hope. Ann Arbor, Mich.: University of Michigan Press, 1960.
———. *Nicomachean Ethics*. Trans. David Ross. New York: Oxford University Press, 1980.
———. *Nicomachean Ethics*. Trans. Terence Irwin. Indianapolis: Hackett, 1985.
———. *Poetics*. In *Aristotle on Poetry and Style*, trans. G.M.A. Grube. Indianapolis: Bobbs-Merrill, 1958.
———. *The Politics*. Trans. T. A. Sinclair. New York: Penguin, 1981.
Austin, J. L. *Philosophical Papers*. Ed. J. O. Urmson and G. J. Warnock. New York: Oxford University Press, 1970.
———. *Sense and Sensibilia*. Ed. G. J. Warnock. New York: Oxford University Press, 1979.
Ayer, A. J. *Language, Truth, and Logic*. New York: Dover, 1952.
Baier, Annette. "Doing Without Moral Theory?" In *Anti-Theory in Ethics and Moral Conservatism,* ed. Stanley G. Clarke and Evan Simpson. Albany: State University of New York Press, 1989.

Benhabib, Seyla, Judith Butler, Drucilla Cornell, and Nancy Fraser. *Feminist Contentions: A Philosophical Exchange*. New York: Routledge, 1995.

Benjamin, Walter. *Illuminations: Essays and Reflections*. Trans. Harry Zohn. New York: Harcourt, Brace & World, 1968.

Berkeley, George. *Three Dialogues Between Hylas and Philonous*. Ed. Robert Merrihew Adams. Indianapolis: Hackett, 1979.

Bernasconi, Robert. "Heidegger's Destruction of Phronesis." *Southern Journal of Philosophy* 28, supplement (Spindel Conference, 1989): 127–47.

Broadie, Sarah. *Ethics with Aristotle*. New York: Oxford University Press, 1991.

Caputo, John. *Against Ethics*. Bloomington: Indiana University Press, 1993.

Card, Claudia. *Lesbian Choices*. New York: Columbia University Press, 1995.

Clarke, Stanley G., and Evan Simpson, eds. *Anti-Theory in Ethics and Moral Conservatism*. Albany: State University of New York Press, 1989.

Code, Lorraine. *What Can She Know?* Ithaca, N.Y.: Cornell University Press, 1991.

Cornell, Drucilla. "From the Lighthouse: The Promise of Redemption and the Possibility of Legal Interpretation." *Cardozo Law Review* 11, nos. 5–6 (1990): 1687–714.

———. *The Philosophy of the Limit*. New York: Routledge, 1992.

Crowther, Paul. *The Kantian Sublime: From Morality to Art*. New York: Oxford University Press, 1989.

Derrida, Jacques. *Dissemination*. Trans. Barbara Johnson. Chicago: University of Chicago Press, 1981.

———. *The Gift of Death*. Trans. David Wills. Chicago: University of Chicago Press, 1995.

———. *Given Time: I, Counterfeit Money*. Trans. Peggy Kamuf. Chicago: University of Chicago Press, 1992.

———. *Margins of Philosophy*. Trans. Alan Bass. Chicago: University of Chicago Press, 1982.

———. *Memoirs of the Blind: The Self-Portrait and Other Ruins*. Trans. Pascale-Anne Brault and Michael Naas. Chicago: University of Chicago Press, 1993.

———. *On the Name*. Ed. Thomas Dutoit. Stanford: Stanford University Press, 1995.

———. *Specters of Marx*. Trans. Peggy Kamuf. New York: Routledge, 1994.

———. *Writing and Difference*. Trans. Alan Bass. Chicago: University of Chicago Press, 1978.

Descartes, Rene. *The Philosophical Works of Descartes*. 2 vols. Trans. Elizabeth S. Haldane and G.R.T. Ross. New York: Cambridge University Press, 1931.

Dreyfus, Hubert L., and Stuart E. Dreyfus. "What Is Morality? A Phenomenological Account of the Development of Ethical Expertise." In *Universalism vs. Communitarianism*, ed. David Rasmussen. Cambridge, Mass.: MIT Press, 1990.

French, Peter A., Theodore E. Uehling Jr., and Howard K. Wettstein, eds. *Midwest Studies in Philosophy, Volume XIII—Ethical Theory: Character and Virtue*. Notre Dame, Ind.: University of Notre Dame Press, 1988.

Gadamer, Hans-Georg. *Truth and Method*. 2d ed. Trans. Joel Weinsheimer and Donald G. Marshall. New York: Crossroad Press, 1989.

Gilligan, Carol. *In a Different Voice*. Cambridge, Mass.: Harvard University Press, 1982.
Giraudoux, Jean. *Giraudoux: La Folle de Chaillot* and *L'Apollon de Bellac*. New York: Dell, 1963.
———. *La Guerre de Troie n'aura pas lieu*. Paris: Le Livre de Poche, 1935.
———. *The Madwoman of Chaillot*. Adapted by Maurice Valency. New York: Dramatists Play Service, 1947.
———. *Tiger at the Gates*. Trans. Christopher Frye. New York: Samuel French, 1956.
Hartsock, Nancy C.M. "The Feminist Standpoint: Developing the Ground for a Specifically Feminist Historical Materialism." In *Discovering Reality*, ed. Sandra Harding and Merrill B. Hintikka. Dordrecht: D. Reidel, 1983.
Hegel, G.W.F. *The Encyclopaedia Logic*. Trans. T. F. Geraets, W. A. Suchting, and H. S. Harris. Indianapolis: Hackett, 1991.
———. *Introduction to the Philosophy of History*. Trans. Leo Rauch. Indianapolis: Hackett, 1988.
Heidegger, Martin. *Aristotle's "Metaphysics" Theta 1–3*. Trans. Walter Brogan and Peter Warnek. Bloomington: Indiana University Press, 1995.
———. *The Basic Problems of Phenomenology*. Trans. Albert Hofstadter. Bloomington: Indiana University Press, 1982.
———. *Basic Writings*. Trans. David Farrell Krell. New York: Harper, 1993.
———. *Being and Time*. Trans. John Macquarrie and Edward Robinson. New York: Harper, 1962.
———. *On Time and Being*. Trans. Joan Stambaugh. New York: Harper, 1972.
———. *Plato's "Sophist."* Trans. Richard Rojcewicz and Andre Schuwer. Bloomington: Indiana University Press, 1997.
———. *Poetry, Language, Thought*. Trans. Albert Hofstadter. New York: Harper, 1975.
———. *The Principle of Reason*. Trans. Reginald Lilly. Bloomington: Indiana University Press, 1991.
———. *The Question Concerning Technology*. Trans. William Lovitt. New York: Harper, 1977.
Hoagland, Sarah Lucia. *Lesbian Ethics: Toward New Value*. Palo Alto, Calif.: Institute of Lesbian Studies, 1988.
Holland, Nancy J. *Is Women's Philosophy Possible?* Savage, Md.: Rowman & Littlefield, 1990.
———. "The Opinions of Men and Women: Toward a Different Configuration of Moral Voices." *Journal of Social Philosophy* 24, no. 1 (1993): 65–80.
———. "The Theory/Practice Distinction Shows Up in Practice: Some Thoughts on Epistemology and the Law." *European Journal of Law, Philosophy, and Computer Science* 1–1 (1998): 49–57.
———, ed. *Feminist Interpretations of Jacques Derrida*. University Park: Pennsylvania State University Press, 1997.
Hume, David. *An Enquiry Concerning Human Understanding*. Ed. Eric Steinberg. Indianapolis: Hackett, 1977.
———. *Hume's Enquiries*. Ed. L. A. Selby-Bigge. New York: Oxford University Press, 1975.
———. *A Treatise of Human Nature*. Ed. L. A. Selby-Bigge. New York: Oxford University Press, 1975.
Imbo, Samuel Oluoch. "The Special Political Responsibilities of African Philosophers." *International Studies in Philosophy* 29, no. 1 (1997): 55–67.

Irigaray, Luce. *This Sex Which Is Not One.* Trans. Catherine Porter. Ithaca, N.Y.: Cornell University Press, 1985.
Irwin, T. H. *Aristotle's First Principles.* New York: Cambridge University Press, 1988.
Jaggar, Alison M. "Feminist Ethics." In *Encyclopedia of Ethics,* ed. Lawrence Becker, with Charlotte Becker. New York: Garland, 1992.
———. *Feminist Politics and Human Nature.* Totowa, N.J.: Rowman & Allanheld, 1983.
Kant, Immanuel. *Critique of Judgment.* Trans. Werner S. Pluhar. Indianapolis: Hackett, 1987.
———. *Critique of Practical Reason.* Trans. Lewis White Beck. New York: Macmillan, 1956.
———. *Grounding for the Metaphysics of Morals.* Trans. James W. Ellington. Indianapolis: Hackett, 1981.
———. *The Metaphysics of Morals.* Trans. Mary Gregor. Philadelphia: University of Pennsylvania Press, 1964.
———. *Prolegomena for Any Future Metaphysics.* Trans. James W. Ellington. Indianapolis: Hackett, 1977.
Lévi-Strauss, Claude. *The Elementary Structures of Kinship.* Trans. James Harle Bell, John Richard von Sturmer, and Rodney Needham. Boston: Beacon Press, 1969.
———. *The Savage Mind.* Translation unattributed. Chicago: University of Chicago Press, 1966.
Locke, John. *An Essay Concerning Human Understanding.* Ed. John W. Yolton. 2 vols. New York: Dutton, 1961.
Lyotard, Jean-François. *The Differend: Phrases in Dispute.* Trans. Georges Van Den Abbeele. Minneapolis: University of Minnesota Press, 1988.
MacIntyre, Alasdair. "The Relationship of Philosophy to History." In *After Philosophy: End or Transformation?* ed. Kenneth Baynes, James Bohman, and Thomas McCarthy. Cambridge, Mass.: MIT Press, 1987.
———. "Relativism, Power, and Philosophy." In *After Philosophy: End or Transformation?* ed. Kenneth Baynes, James Bohman, and Thomas McCarthy. Cambridge, Mass.: MIT Press, 1987.
———. "Sōphrosunē: How a Virtue Can Become Socially Disruptive." In *Midwest Studies in Philosophy, Volume XIII—Ethical Theory: Character and Virtue,* ed. Peter A. French, Theodore E. Uehling Jr., and Howard K. Wettstein. Notre Dame, Ind.: University of Notre Dame Press, 1988.
Mahowald, Mary Briody, ed. *Philosophy of Woman.* Indianapolis: Hackett, 1983.
Makkreel, Rudolf. *Imagination and Interpretation in Kant.* Chicago: University of Chicago Press, 1990.
Marx, Karl. *Selected Writings.* Ed. David McLellan. New York: Oxford University Press, 1977.
Matsuo, Hiroshi. "Historical and Theoretical Intimacy Between the Concepts of Rights and Property." *European Journal of Law, Philosophy, and Computer Science* 3 (1995) (*17th IVR World Congress—"Challenges to Law at the End of the 20th Century"*): 11–17.
McBrien, Richard P. *Catholicism.* Minneapolis, Minn.: Winston Press, 1981.
Mill, John Stuart. *On Liberty.* Ed. Elizabeth Rapaport. Indianapolis: Hackett, 1978.

———. *Utilitarianism.* Ed. George Sher. Indianapolis: Hackett, 1979.
Minh-ha, Trinh T. Introduction to *Discourse* 8 (fall-winter 1986–87): 3–9.
Moraga, Cherríe. "From a Long Line of Vendidas: Chicanas and Feminism." Excerpted in *Feminist Frameworks,* ed. Alison M. Jaggar and Paula S. Rothenberg. New York: McGraw-Hill, 1993. (From Moraga's *Loving in the War Years: Lo que nunca paso por sus labios* [Boston: South End Press, 1983].)
Murray, Gilbert. *Five Stages of Greek Religion.* Garden City, N.Y.: Doubleday, 1951.
New Catholic Encyclopedia. New York: McGraw-Hill, 1967.
Nietzsche, Friedrich. *The Portable Nietzsche.* Trans. and ed. Walter Kaufmann. New York: Viking, 1968.
Nussbaum, Martha. *The Fragility of Goodness: Luck and Ethics in Greek Tragedy and Philosophy.* New York: Cambridge University Press, 1986.
———. "Non-Relative Virtues: An Aristotelian Approach." In *Midwest Studies in Philosophy, Volume XIII—Ethical Theory: Character and Virtue,* ed. Peter A. French, Theodore E. Uehling Jr., and Howard K. Wettstein. Notre Dame, Ind.: University of Notre Dame Press, 1988.
O'Neill, H. C. *New Things and Old in Saint Thomas Aquinas.* London: Dent & Co., 1909.
O'Neill, Onora. *Constructions of Reason: Explorations of Kant's Practical Philosophy.* New York: Cambridge University Press, 1989.
Plato. *The Dialogues of Plato.* Trans. Benjamin Jowett. New York: Random House, 1937.
———. *Gorgias.* Trans. Donald J. Zeyl. Indianapolis: Hackett, 1987.
Polk, Timothy. "In the Image: Aesthetics and Ethics Through the Glass of Scripture." *Horizons in Biblical Theology* 8 (1986): 27–59.
Rice, Donald, and Peter Schofer. *Rhetorical Poetics.* Madison: University of Wisconsin Press, 1983.
Rorty, Richard. *Contingency, Irony, and Solidarity.* New York: Cambridge University Press, 1989.
———. "Solidarity or Objectivity?" In *Anti-Theory in Ethics and Moral Conservatism,* ed. Stanley G. Clarke and Evan Simpson. Albany: State University of New York Press, 1989.
Rubin, Gayle. "The Traffic in Women." In *Toward an Anthropology of Women,* ed. Rayna R. Reiter. New York: Monthly Review Press, 1975.
Ruether, Rosemary Radford. *Sexism and God-Talk: Toward a Feminist Theology.* Boston: Beacon Press, 1983.
———, ed. *Religion and Sexism.* New York: Simon & Schuster, 1974.
Schott, Robin May. *Cognition and Eros: A Critique of the Kantian Paradigm.* Boston: Beacon Press, 1988.
Scott, Charles E. *The Question of Ethics.* Bloomington: Indiana University Press, 1990.
Searle, John. *Speech Acts.* New York: Cambridge University Press, 1969.
Serequeberhan, Tsenay. *The Hermeneutics of African Philosophy: Horizon and Discourse.* New York: Routledge, 1994.
Sherman, Nancy. "Common Sense and Uncommon Virtue." In *Midwest Studies in Philosophy, Volume XIII—Ethical Theory: Character and Virtue,* ed. Peter A. French, Theodore E. Uehling Jr., and Howard K. Wettstein. Notre Dame, Ind.: University of Notre Dame Press, 1988.
———. *The Fabric of Character.* New York: Oxford University Press, 1989.

Solomon, David. "Internal Objections to Virtue Ethics." In *Midwest Studies in Philosophy, Volume XIII—Ethical Theory: Character and Virtue,* ed. Peter A. French, Theodore E. Uehling Jr., and Howard K. Wettstein. Notre Dame, Ind.: University of Notre Dame Press, 1988.

Spivak, Gayatri Chakravorty. "Displacement and the Discourse of Woman." In *Feminist Interpretations of Jacques Derrida,* ed. Nancy J. Holland. University Park: Pennsylvania State University Press, 1997.

———. "Ghostwriting." *diacritics* 25 (summer 1995): 65–84.

Swidler, Leonard, and Arlene Swidler, eds. *Women Priests: A Catholic Commentary on the Vatican Declaration.* New York: Paulist Press, 1977.

Taylor, Charles. *The Ethics of Authenticity.* Cambridge, Mass.: Harvard University Press, 1991.

Tong, Rosemarie. *Feminine and Feminist Ethics.* Belmont, Calif.: Wadsworth, 1993.

Williams, Bernard. *Shame and Necessity.* Berkeley and Los Angeles: University of California Press, 1993.

Williams, Patricia. *The Alchemy of Race and Rights: Diary of a Law Professor.* Cambridge, Mass.: Harvard University Press, 1991.

Wiredu, Kwasi. *Cultural Universals and Particulars: An African Perspective.* Bloomington: Indiana University Press, 1996.

Wittgenstein, Ludwig. *On Certainty.* Ed. G.E.M. Anscombe and G. H. von Wright. Trans. Denis Paul and G.E.M. Anscombe. New York: Harper, 1972.

Index

Adorno, Theodor, 85–86, 88
alethēia. *See* Truth
Allison, Henry, 50–52
Aristotle, xvii, xxx–xxxi, 4, 10, 16–20, 24–30, 32–45, 47–48, 51–57, 62–65, 68–69, 71–80, 85, 89, 97, 102, 107–9
Austin, J. L., xxii–xxiii, xxvii, 30n
authenticity. See *Eigentlichkeit*

Baier, Annette, 100–104
Berkeley, George, xx–xxi, xxiv, 31
Broadie, Sarah, 35n, 36n, 38–44, 73

Card, Claudia, 72, 92n, 95–99, 104, 110
"care" ethics, xv, 92, 106
Cornell, Drucilla, xii–xiii(n), xxiv(n), 15n, 71, 85–95, 104, 110
critical legal studies, 85, 93–95
Crowther, Paul, 50

Darwin, Charles, xxviii
"Declaration on the Question of the Admission of Women to the Ministerial Priesthood," 60–61, 64–67
Derrida, Jacques, xxvii–xxviii, xxx, 1–2, 10–19, 23, 79, 82, 85–89, 94, 100n, 108–10
Descartes, René, xix–xx, xxiv, 31, 35, 46
Dickens, Charles, 82
Dostoyevksy, Fyodor, xxv
Dreyfus, Hubert, 79, 106–7

Eigentlichkeit (authenticity), 2–3, 5–12
Einstein, Albert, xxviii
Ereignis (event), 2–4, 6–7, 11–12, 17
Euripides, 107

feminism, xv, xxix, xxx, 3n, 9, 14–17, 22, 55–56, 71–72, 82, 84–85, 91–99
Foucault, Michel, xv

Index

Freud, Sigmund, xxviii–xxix, 80–81, 84

Gadamer, Hans-Georg, 19n, 21, 40, 42n, 59, 70, 89, 107n
Gilligan, Carol, 92, 106
Giraudoux, Jean, xi–xvi, xxii, xxvii, 16, 20, 27, 83–84, 91, 94, 97–99, 110

Habermas, Jürgen, 82, 85
Hegel, G. W. F., xxiv–xxviii, 6, 11, 85, 109
Heidegger, Martin, xviii(n), xxix–xxx, 1–18, 20–22, 35, 39, 44–45, 50, 79, 82, 85–87, 101–6, 110
Hoagland, Sarah Lucia, 97–98
Hobbes, Thomas, 31
Hofstadter, Albert, 3–4, 6, 105
Homer, 74
Hume, David, xxi–xxiii, xxv, 15, 31, 45–49, 54n, 56, 67n, 75, 78, 100–102
Husserl, Edmund, 11

Irwin, Terence, 18, 35n, 37–44, 49, 73

Jaggar, Alison, ix, xx(n), 91
justice, 13, 17–19, 21, 29–30, 33, 44, 87, 89–90, 97; vs. "care" ethics, xv, 92

Kant, Immanuel, xvii, xxiii–xxiv, xxvii, xxx–xxxi, 10, 20, 22, 24–28, 33, 39, 42–57, 67–68, 71, 73, 78, 80, 85, 87, 102, 107–8
Kierkegaard, Søren, 2, 25, 109

Lacan, Jacques, 85, 88
Lévi-Strauss, Claude, xxvi, 14n
Levinas, Immanuel, 85, 87, 109
Locke, John, xix–xxi, xxiv
logical positivism, xxii, xxvi–xxvii
Lovitt, William, 4, 7
Lyotard, Jean-François, xvii–xviii, xxix–xxx(n), 50

MacIntyre, Alasdair, 71, 73–75, 78, 103
Madwoman of Chaillot, The, xi–xvii, xix, xxvi–xxviii, 8, 13, 15, 44, 56–58, 83–84, 90–91, 94, 97–99, 103–4, 106–7, 109–10
Makkreel, Rudolf, 49–50
Mapplethorpe, Robert, 106–7

Marx, Karl, xv, xxv, xxvii, 10, 12–15, 55
marxism, xiii, xxii, xxv–xxvi, 21
McBrien, Richard P., 60, 64–66, 68
Mill, John Stuart, xxi, xxviii(n), 24–29, 31–33, 36–37, 40, 46, 56, 68n, 80–82, 84
Murray, Gilbert, 18

Nabokov, Vladimir, 82
"naturalistic fallacy," xxi, 31
Nietzsche, Friedrich, xv, xxv–xxvi, 16n, 28, 81–82, 96
Nussbaum, Martha, 43–44, 71, 76–79, 82, 92, 104, 110

Ockham, William of, xviii
O'Neill, H. C., 61
O'Neill, Onora, 51–52
ordination of women, xxx, 59–70, 77, 82, 90, 95

Patočka, Jan, 109
Paul, Saint, 61–62, 64–65, 68
phronēsis (practical wisdom), xix, 17, 19, 99
Piaget, Jean, xxvi
Plato, xvii, 24–34, 36–37, 40–41, 45–46, 55–57, 68, 74, 80
present-at-hand (*Vorhandenheit*), 5, 8–9, 11, 102–7, 109
Proust, Marcel, 82
Putnam, Hilary, 82

Rawls, John, 82, 85
ready-to-hand (*Zuhandenheit*), 5, 8, 101–6
Reuther, Rosemary Radford, 61n, 66
Rorty, Richard, 71, 79–85, 88–89, 91, 104

Sartre, Jean-Paul, xxvi
Schott, Robin, 55–56
Scotus, Duns, xviii
Serequeberhan, Tsenay, 21–22
Sherman, Nancy, 41, 77
Socrates, 2, 18, 25, 28–30, 32
Solomon, David, 72–73, 78
sōphrosunē (temperance), 17–20, 41, 51–52, 74–75, 79, 90, 99, 102–3, 105
Spinoza, Baruch, xxiv, 48, 56
Stroud, Barry, 101
structuralism, xxvi–xxvii, 14

Thomas Aquinas, 61–63, 65, 69–70, 75, 78, 102
Tiger at the Gates (*La Guerre de Troie n'aura pas lieu*), xiv, 20, 99
Tong, Rosemarie, 91–92, 95, 99n
truth (*aletheia*), 5, 8, 105–6

unready-to-hand (*Unzuhandenheit*), 5, 8, 102–7, 109

utilitarianism, xiv, xvii, xxi–xxii, xxv–xxvi, 24, 27–33, 56, 78

Williams, Bernard, 16n, 20, 35
Williams, Patricia, 72, 93–95, 97–99, 104, 110
Wiredu, Kwasi, 21–22, 53–54, 104n
Wittgenstein, Ludwig, xxii–xxiii, 96

NANCY J. HOLLAND is Professor of Philosophy at Hamline University in Saint Paul, Minnesota. She is the author of *Is Women's Philosophy Possible?* (Rowmand and Littlefield, 1990) and editor of *Feminist Interpretations of Jacques Derrida* (Penn State, 1997).

www.ingramcontent.com/pod-product-compliance
Lightning Source LLC
Chambersburg PA
CBHW031553300426
44111CB00006BA/300